No News Is Bad News

Also by Ian Gill

Hiking on the Edge: Canada's West Coast Trail

*Haida Gwaii: Journeys Through the Queen
Charlotte Islands*

*All That We Say Is Ours: Guujaaw and the
Reawakening of the Haida Nation*

Canada's Media Collapse—
and What Comes Next

IAN GILL

Foreword by **MARGO GOODHAND**

DAVID SUZUKI INSTITUTE

 GREYSTONE BOOKS
Vancouver/Berkeley

For Heather...

... always far, forever dear

Greystone Books Ltd.

www.greystonebooks.com

David Suzuki Institute

219-2211 West 4th Avenue

Vancouver BC Canada V6K 4S2

Cataloguing data available from Library and Archives Canada

ISBN 978-1-77164-268-2 (pbk.)

ISBN 978-1-77164-269-9 (epub)

Editing by Eva van Emden

Copy-editing by Amanda Growe

Cover design by Will Brown

Text design by Nayeli Jimenez

Printed and bound in Canada on ancient-forest-friendly paper by Friesens

Image credits: Page 1: by Ed Stein for *Rocky Mountain News*, 2008. Page 44: Communications Management Inc., "Canada's Digital Divides," August 20, 2015. Page 72: Madelaine Drohan, "Does serious journalism have a future in Canada?" Public Policy Forum, March 2016, 10, adapted from Canadian Media Concentration Research Project, "Media and Internet Concentration in Canada Report, 1984–2014," November 2015. Page 127: by David Beers, unpublished, 2016.

We gratefully acknowledge the support of the Canada Council for the Arts, the British Columbia Arts Council, the Province of British Columbia through the Book Publishing Tax Credit, and the Government of Canada for our publishing activities.

CONTENTS

WHO IS TELLING Canada's stories? Does anybody care? Why should we?

A lot of Canadians are looking for answers these days as the nation's newsrooms rapidly diminish.

With corporate concentration at an all-time high and those few owners challenged by plummeting ad revenues and an obsolete business model, the long-term outlook for traditional media in Canada has never looked so grim.

Print and broadcast media have been shedding journalists over the past decade or so, but the situation was never so stark as it became in 2015, as the debt-laden Postmedia, which already owned most of Canada's major daily newspapers, borrowed more money to buy up the equally challenged Sun Media chain of more than 170 smaller dailies and weeklies.

By early 2016, despite the massive and uncontested takeover, Postmedia teetered on the brink of bankruptcy. Breaking its own vows to keep its newsrooms separate and competitive, the company laid off dozens more journalists (including me, and with more to follow), and merged Sun and Postmedia newsrooms in Edmonton, Ottawa, Vancouver, and Calgary.

Into the middle of this mess cheerfully wandered writer and social entrepreneur Ian Gill, a former print and broadcast journalist at the *Vancouver Sun* and the CBC, and currently a regular columnist for the *Tyee*.

Gill set off to explore how other countries—from Italy to the UK to Australia to the US—are coping with the inevitable erosion of mainstream media in this digital age, and what is starting to emerge in its place.

He talked to insiders and innovators, and in this intelligent and highly opinionated critique offers keen insights into today's media landscape, and better yet, hope for the future.

There are no sacred cows in his lively and engaging analysis, which takes on everyone from the CBC to the *Globe and Mail* in a breezy style which will make you laugh, wince, and most importantly think.

His assessment rings true, particularly for those who, like me, have lived through the slow, shuddering decline of the Canwest and then the Postmedia/Sun Media empires. But it also goes further than a number of recent books and articles on this topic, specifically seeking out a wide variety of experts on the latest and most promising forms of media.

Other countries, Gill notes, have successfully made a head start with new and economically viable models, even as Canada remains "stuck in a decade-old holding pattern" of aging (and listing) media corporations.

He makes the point that it is clearly time to shake off the status quo, but he also never loses sight of his core principle: that a healthy media makes a healthy democracy.

No News Is Bad News is essential reading for anyone who wants to better understand how we got here, where we're headed, and maybe, just maybe, how we might make things better.

—MARGO GOODHAND

Margo Goodhand is the former editor of the *Edmonton Journal* and the *Winnipeg Free Press*, and most recently the author of Above the Fold on TheWalrus.ca, a look at the state of Canada's newspaper industry.

INTRODUCTION

Requiem mass media

FIGURE 1. Pillars of salt: One year after this cartoon was published, Denver's *Rocky Mountain News* closed its doors, two months shy of its 150th birthday. (*Rocky Mountain News*)

That giant sucking sound

THAT GIANT SUCKING sound you hear? Oh, that's just the implosion of Canadian media. Shame about that. You'd think someone would have done something. True, there have only been a few telltale signs, things like the ritual slashing of the country's journalistic workforce and the erasure of billions of dollars of shareholder value from large media companies. There have been spectacularly ill-advised media mergers, especially in broadcasting and newspaper publishing. Media ownership has become so concentrated it's a wonder your newspaper or television broadcast doesn't come with a health warning. And then there's that darned thing called the Internet.

Canadian media industries are collapsing. Newspapers have been particularly hard hit. Once-venerable papers, some as long-lived as Confederation, have closed outright. Those that survive are shadows of their former selves, their newsrooms gutted, their content mostly worthless. All this has happened under the noses of regulators who don't do their jobs and reporters who mostly don't do theirs, either— at least if the job of a reporter is to help people make sense of the world, including their own corner of it. In the meantime, the owners and investors—they too have failed us, being far too slow and dull-witted to have seen, let alone responded to, the massive disruptions that the Internet has wrought on media the world over.

We are just now waking up to how badly Canadians have been caught off-guard by the global media revolution, and how much it affects us all. The hollowing out of Canada's media is bad for democracy, and it runs counter to the claim that in the post–Stephen Harper era, Canada is somehow "back." Actually, we have become a media backwater, and it is going to get a lot worse before it gets better.

For me, a former newspaper journalist, what is happening to Canada's newspaper industry feels personal, which might partly explain why my distress at the parlous state of Canadian newspapers veers towards the intemperate. I feel like we are being robbed blind, mugged by the oligarchs, and fed a diet of content you wouldn't serve in a hospital during a power outage.

I worked in newspapers for about a dozen years in all, both in my native Australia and here in Canada, and I loved the work. My first newspaper was a triweekly called the *Whyalla News*. Whyalla was a hard country town in South Australia, stinking hot most of the time, an industrial outpost of mostly immigrant workers who built ships and smelted iron ore. The *Whyalla News* was an incorrigible civic booster. Once I figured out what a reporter was supposed to do (I never went to college and was hired pretty much off the street on the strength of a somewhat fictional resumé typed by my girlfriend at the time), I had some early scrapes with the editor—me trying to get stories printed that rattled the municipal cage, and him succeeding in watering them down or keeping them out of the paper altogether.

It was an amazing—if sometimes discouraging—learning opportunity for me, and for the owners of the *Whyalla*

News, it was a good business. The company ran a large printing press, mixing outside commercial print jobs with print runs of the *News.* This was in the days of hot lead, with compositors setting type line by line. When I finished my reporting shift, I would go into the shop. I loved the smell and the clatter of the place, and I was fascinated by the skill and speed with which the compositors would set type. I would stick around to watch the first papers come off the press. I thrilled every time at the realization that I could write something up in the newsroom and soon afterwards, through a complex series of social and technological navigations, everything from front-page stories to sports scores and the shipping news would end up on page after page that people would pay money for. It seemed like the work of alchemists.

I was a cub reporter earning almost nothing. So I couldn't afford to, but I wrote away to Hatchards, one of the oldest bookstores in the UK, and in exchange for a fantastic amount of money, they sent me the five volumes of *Editing and Design* by legendary *Sunday Times* editor Harold Evans. Book 1: *Newsman's English.* Book 2: *Handling Newspaper Text.* Book 3: *News Headlines.* Book 4: *Picture Editing.* Book 5: *Newspaper Design.* I have them still, in their impossibly luxe dust covers. I pored over them then, schooling myself in a kind of no man's land between the high-mindedness of Evans and the low practice of covering agricultural field days in far-flung Australian country towns. I loved every bit of newspapering, including my shorthand teacher, as it happens. I quickly moved on to a bigger paper in Perth, and after a year there, spent two years covering Parliament in Canberra.

When I moved to Canada and got hired at the *Vancouver Sun* in the early '80s, the transition to computers was underway, but the Pacific Press building at 2250 Granville Street was still anchored by a massive printing press. After the paper had gone to bed, but before I did, I would sometimes hang around the back shop watching the paginators do their thing, and just like in Whyalla, I would go down to the press room and watch huge newsprint rolls take their turn at hosting the day's news. Compared to the quiet clicking of the newsroom, the press room was so muscular, so thunderous. All this to say that when it comes to being sentimental about newspapers, I've got form.

When I worked for the *Sun*, the paper was okay, but just okay. Even then, reporters reminisced about the good old days. The *Sun* was a mediocre newspaper in the 1980s, but while those days were very far from halcyon, they seem utterly brilliant compared to the pallor of today's iteration. Then, at least, the *Sun* was not the utter embarrassment to the city that it is today.

After seven years as an editor and reporter, I quit the *Sun* to join CBC TV in 1988. That posting deserves its own nostalgic affection, even if those weren't brilliant times for TV broadcasting either, because my gig was actually pretty good while it lasted. I got to do documentaries about important issues and, in particular, was privileged to travel

to the far corners of British Columbia and interview Canadians, especially First Nations people, whose voices were
otherwise unheard in our national discourse. It felt then
that we were performing a very real and very distinct public service. But after successive funding cutbacks and the
installation of one too many boneheaded executive producers, the CBC simply wasn't fun anymore; I left in 1994
to found an environmental non-profit. But I never lost my
affection for journalism and even, in small doses, journalists. More to the point, I have never lost my belief in the
importance of journalism in public life.

In those so-so days at the *Sun*, I came to resent the fact
that while we started every print run with blank rolls of
newsprint, with a licence to put just about anything we
wanted on those pages, we mostly filled the paper with
garbage. It seemed like such an abuse, such a waste of
everything, the high ideals of journalism lost in second-rate
thinking by owners, then as now beholden to special interests and happy to hire mediocre managers who did their
bidding.

The blood was already starting to drain out of the *Sun*
when I started there in 1981, the same year the Royal Commission on Newspapers reported on the shocking state of
concentration of Canadian newspaper ownership. Like a
number of colleagues actively trying to arrest the decline
of journalism even then, I joined the Centre for Investigative Journalism, becoming its vice-president for a spell,
and I invited Ben Bagdikian—a well-known media critic

who among other things helped the *Washington Post* get hold of and publish the Pentagon Papers—to be a keynote speaker at the CIJ convention in Vancouver in 1986. Three years earlier, he had published a seminal book, *The Media Monopoly.* Across North America, newspaper ownership concentration was seen as a dangerous blight, and Bagdikian chronicled the disease brilliantly. In the intervening decades, sadly, it has only gotten worse.

Chronicle of a death foretold

CANADA'S SLOW-WITTED AND flat-footed media companies have been on the wrong side of history for almost a generation now, and it is really starting to hurt. For more than half my adult life, I have lived in a great and growing city with two lousy and shrivelling newspapers. Most Canadians aren't that lucky—either to live in Vancouver, or to have two newspapers, even bad ones, to choose from. Mostly, when it comes to newspapers, Canadians have no choice: they just take what their one local, lousy legacy rag offers up—or, increasingly, they get no newspaper at all. For the 20 per cent of Canadians, meanwhile, who don't live in cities, the pickings are slimmer, and there's no point arguing about quality because there isn't any.

Then there's television. Or in lots of smaller Canadian markets, there's not, because local original content is too expensive to produce. In larger markets, there is greater variety to be sure, but the television product in this country is mostly so plastic and cosmetic that it's as if the Mattel toy company bought up our media companies to provide jobs for their product line.

Magazines? Not so much. We lost a *Beaver* and got a *Walrus* in exchange, and what's to like about that? Radio? Mostly noisome bingo callers, unless you are among the legions of Canadians who have had their brains cryogenically suspended in the gelid slush of Stuart McLean's so-called storytelling in his *Vinyl Cafe*. Perhaps that's where to lay the blame for the fact that Canadians have mostly slept through the great unravelling of our national media universe. Dave bastes the turkey while the nation's media are cooked to a crisp.

But hey, look at us—we don't all have blue hair and hearing aids. This is Canada, and we have the World Wide Web! Problem is, journalistically at least, we really don't, because Canada's media companies have been abject failures in intelligently responding to a digital revolution that began before the turn of this century and has utterly disrupted our media landscape in the decade and a half since.

It is nearing the point that, just as our biosphere is widely thought to be entering a new geologic epoch, the Anthropocene—coinciding with a sixth mass extinction of the Earth's species—our mediasphere is careening towards what might be thought of as a Sixth Estate, with a corresponding die-off of our media diversity—or at least our media dinosaurs.

As a Commonwealth country, Canada has long laboured under the comfortable assumption that our three main estates—the Church and our two houses of Parliament—are counterbalanced by the institutional gravity and probity of our mainstream media, the so-called Fourth Estate. The advent of the Internet ushered in what came to be known as the Fifth Estate.* The media status quo was quickly overtaken by a less mediated and vastly more disaggregated arena of bloggers and hacktivists, unfettered by the norms of traditional journalism, who have revelled in a new-found freedom to express outlier, often subversive, sometimes cranky or outlandish views—sometimes brilliant work, too—that never would have made it into a mainstream newspaper or broadcast. Social media emerged as an everyman's latter-day carrier pigeon for releasing whatever thought was top of mind—no matter whose mind or how well-formed a thought. This mostly dumbing down, although some might call it a democratization, of our media has been decried as unhealthy—all sound and fury, signifying nothing.

To some extent, that anxiety is not misplaced. Whether mediated through a Fourth, Fifth, or perhaps now a Sixth Estate—or more radically, not mediated at all—any society that aspires to be taken seriously as a developed, democratic, pluralistic, well-governed, innovative, and creative force in the world—and isn't that what Canada wants above all, to be a positive force in the world?—needs a journalistic environment that is healthy, exciting, and diverse.

---

* Not to be confused, in Canada, with *The Fifth Estate*, a cleverly named and admirably executed CBC documentary television show that is very much a product of mainstream journalism at its best.

Canada's is the opposite of that: moribund, flaccid, and as glabrous as Peter Mansbridge's pate. The blame lies less with the rapid disruptions wrought by new technology and instead with complacent owners, tremulous investors, and inattentive regulators, whose failure to recognize what is happening to media business models has been exacerbated by soft-minded journalists, who have largely missed the story of their own demise. It's as if Canada's journalists were assigned to cover a state funeral, and only now are wising up to the fact that the body in the casket is their own.

JOURNALISTS AREN'T EASY to love. They are less trusted than police, schools, banks, and the justice system, and only marginally more trusted than federal Parliament and corporations.[1] But what journalists do is important, and it isn't just the business of rooting out liars, holding policy-makers accountable, probing the public accounts, championing the underdogs, or hounding the overlords. It is all of those things, but it is more importantly the practice of using stories as a way to help people make sense of their world.

It is not enough to write the first draft of history. The job of journalism is also to recall and reflect on our shared history, to capture or at least help channel the currents of our times, and to help us imagine what sort of society we wish to invent for ourselves and for those who come after us. Yes, debates happen in this country's legislatures, our rules of conduct are enforced in our courts, and our commerce is carried out, sometimes in public, often in private, and most of the system works for most of the people most of the time. But not always, and not for everybody—which is why our public square needs to include spaces where we can challenge the status quo, encourage dissent, listen at the margins, and champion new ideas, new ways of doing things, new ways of seeing the world, new ways of understanding our place in it. We need new places to share those stories in multiple and evolving ways.

To do all that, good journalism needs a home, *many* homes actually, but in Canada we've failed to keep our media house in order, and our public square is shrinking fast. Canadian journalism is on life-support—not because Canadian reporters don't know how to do journalism, but because there are so few places to put it anymore. We've clung for so long to dinosaur media-business models that while pretty much everyone else in the developed world is driving the journalistic version of a Tesla these days, here we are all crammed into a second-hand Edsel, wondering if we can afford snow tires.

How did things get so bad? Will they get worse? Should we even care anymore? And if so, what should we do about it?

Someone once said that the environment is too important to leave to environmentalists, and the same could be said about journalism. If it is true that as many as ten thousand journalism jobs in Canada have disappeared in less than a decade,[2] then arguably there aren't enough journalists around anymore to report themselves missing, and the good ones who have survived thus far are likely to be hopelessly conflicted when it comes to taking proper account of the businesses that generate their paycheques. Veteran reporter Paul Watson has said that Canada's big media companies, or "legacy media," have become "old, slow, and lazy" and that Canadian journalists have essentially missed the story, focusing on the changing media landscape as a technology issue, rather than holding their owners, and themselves, to account. "Journalists are very good at putting the heat on other people... but they're very bad at turning the heat on themselves."[3] As such, they have been complicit in their own demise.

With rare exceptions, such as Jesse Brown's *Canadaland* podcast and website, there's a lack of thoughtful reporting on what's happening in our media. True, media closures (and the occasional opening) are routinely covered in what's left of our media, and certainly what's happening to the business produces plenty of hand-wringing at journalism conferences. Then there's the dutiful quarterly reporting, really a death watch, over Postmedia's latest losses. Or there's an occasional splenetic outburst like we heard early in 2016 from the head of the Canadian Radio-television and Telecommunications Commission (CRTC), who scolded television executives for crying poor from the sterns of their luxury yachts or the seats of their private helicopters.[4] But let's just say that critiques of Canadian media, when left to Canadian media, don't exactly brim with honest self-reflection.

When they have been stirred to respond to the crisis unfolding under their very noses, the response has been to plump for a demoralizingly nostalgic and insipid campaign that Unifor, Ryerson University, and a few media companies launched in 2015 called JournalismIS,[5] which sounds like nothing so much as a drunken reporter about to fall off her stool at the National Press Club of Canada, except you can't even do that anymore because the press club went bankrupt and shut its doors in 2007. JournalismIS, we are told, "essential to democracy," "relentless," "committed to the public interest," and a "watchdog over the powerful," and of course in an ideal world that would all be true. But in Canada, it hasn't been true for a very long time. A more accurate campaign would be called JournalismWAS, and it could take its cue from Monty Python—"I'm not dead!"

Journalists? That's the same conclave about which Baron Black of Crossharbour once famously said, "We must express the view, based on our empirical observations, that a substantial number of journalists are ignorant, lazy, opinionated, and intellectually dishonest. The profession is heavily cluttered with aged hacks toiling through a miasma of mounting decrepitude and often alcoholism, and even more so with arrogant and abrasive youngsters who substitute 'commitment' for insight."[6] By that measure, why bother lamenting the loss of a single journalist, let alone an entire *division* of them? When it comes to journalists, who cares if the breed goes extinct? Those *soi-disant* "watchdogs over the powerful" have failed to keep a proper watch

over their own sacred estates, possibly by confusing what
Marshall McLuhan once said about the medium being the
message, contorting themselves into a contented belief that
mediocrity is a message and a medium both—and journalists are its avatars.

And then along comes the Oscar-winning film *Spot-
light* to remind us that, imperfect as journalists may be,
what they do sometimes matters, and sometimes it matters a lot. And Conrad Black should remember that it is
the media proprietors, not the practitioners of journalism—lazy, drunk, or otherwise—who are the real villains
in this piece. There is no shying away from the fact that
it is the owners and publishers who have bankrupted and/
or destroyed the value of Canada's great media companies,
and they've been getting away with it for decades. That, as
much as anything, begins to explain how utterly dreadful
Canadian media have become. Ben Bagdikian once wrote,
"Trying to be a first-rate reporter on the average American newspaper is like trying to play Bach's *St. Matthew
Passion* on a ukulele."[7] Well, the average Canadian newspaper is an instrument that has been stripped so bare that
trying to be even a second-rate reporter in this country is
like being asked to play Céline Dion's "My Heart Will Go
On" on a washboard. You have to wonder if it's even worth
trying.

Should anything be done to rescue Canadian media
from themselves? The question seems to hit home especially hard when it comes to newspapers, because even

though they are very much fading from view as the journalistic vehicle of choice in today's sea of zeros and ones, there remains a belief—maybe just among the *Vinyl Cafe* demographic and former newspaper reporters like me, who remember what a good paper can do—that newspapers have a weight and authority that other media cannot match and never will. They have a "fixity," as one study of print- and computer-based reading describes it, that even good news websites can't match. "The printed page was, to the study group, a cultural object."[8] In Vancouver, which now bills itself as an international city—or certainly it sells its houses at international prices—it wouldn't be the worst thing to have a good newspaper to wake up to every morning. But that's not going to happen anytime soon. Our daily "cultural objects," the *Vancouver Sun* and the *Province*, are less like lanterns illuminating the modern world and more like lava lamps fitted with 20-watt bulbs.

Rider on the storm

SO, WITH MY way largely unlit by any bright lights in domestic mainstream media, in 2015 I embarked on a voyage of discovery about the state of Canadian media that quickly became, with apologies to author Ronald Wright, what one might call *A Short History of Regress*. No longer an industry insider, my time outside of mainstream journalism has given me a more multi-faceted view of the media than being a lifer would ever have allowed, but it carries its limitations. I do not consider myself an industry expert and I'm certainly not an academic, but my detour through the world of conservation, community development, policy advocacy, philanthropy, social entrepreneurship, organizational development, and plowing the fields of social innovation in search of social impact—well, that's not a bad base from which to try to make sense of what's happened to Canadian media.

This is a big industry in a big country and it's not realistic to think that one can get one's arms around it all, so I followed my nose. I was referred to people somewhat opportunistically, I was biased more towards newspapers than television and broadcasting, and I just glanced at magazines. I visited one J-school, not lots. I leaned more towards content than technology. My inquiries focused mostly on English-language models, at home and abroad.

What follows is not just a battlefield casualty report, but a search for solutions. I entered the fray in part with an eye to how philanthropic foundations or mission-focused investors might contribute innovation funding in the media space, as many do in the US. So I spent a good amount of time viewing what I learned through that lens, as opposed to just what is or isn't working in journalism per se.

And finally, who I sought out, who I left out, and the conclusions I drew were informed by my values and my beliefs about what the role of media should be. This includes my discontent with the media status quo and my history of personal advocacy for social change, particularly with respect to environmental and indigenous issues in Canada and abroad. Thus my analysis is inseparable from a basic set of assumptions arising from my experience and personal passions, including the following beliefs:

- Robust, independent, and fearless journalism is essential to the proper, engaged, pluralistic, accountable, and transparent functioning of our democracy. Or, to quote from the Knight Commission on the Information Needs of Communities in a Democracy, news and information are "as vital to the healthy functioning of communities as clean air, safe streets, good schools, and public health."[9]

- Canadian philanthropy is delinquent in its almost total absence of support for good journalism, abdicating what should be a leadership role in enabling widespread and effective dissemination of progressive thought in a country that spent a decade being beaten black and Tory blue by Stephen Harper.

- Progressive organizations and forces have been losing the battle for narrative, and the lack of diverse and independent media constricts the passages through which it is possible to argue for positive social change and policy reform.

- While one would like to think that all journalism is, by definition, public-interest journalism, the fact is that most of it is not, and public-interest journalism has suffered most of all from a combination of spending cuts and the ensuing declines in content and competence in our mainstream media.

- Our ability to help shape a culture of innovation, and to advance transformative change in Canada, is hobbled by the narrowness of a national conversation that is constantly circumscribed by economic and political forces that are the antithesis of a transparent, engaged, and fully functioning democracy.

- It is especially urgent for Canadians to continue and indeed to expand upon the conversation with Aboriginal communities that was started—but by no means finished—by the Truth and Reconciliation Commission.

- With the accelerating urbanization of Canada, rural communities—and especially Aboriginal reserve communities—are hardest hit by the service declines in our media.

- A new, Reconciliation-centric narrative for Canada is unlikely to emerge with anything like the moral and intellectual force that the times demand without a media landscape that reflects the diversity, creativity, and cultural complexity of the country, and the many demands of and on its citizenry.

- Existing media tools for disseminating knowledge and practice—particularly in areas of policy reform, and even more when spotlighting social complexity, poor service delivery, and outright dysfunction—are mostly ill suited to the task.

- Our major newspapers, in particular, are in thrall to big business—energy industries most of all, but also developers, finance industries, and other natural-resource players—sectors that, ironically, are becoming less and less reliable as sources of revenue for media.

To this latter point, it is worth thinking about the extent to which Canada's historically heavy economic dependence on our natural resources has been mirrored by an over-reliance on an unnaturally small pool of large media players. The price of oil plummets and large swaths of the country become economically unviable. Ad revenue drops and the same goes for newsrooms. As go the tar sands, so goes Postmedia. Just as our energy economy has been slow to diversify into more sustainable fuels, the feet of clay of our media economy, especially that of our newspapers, has been ownership concentration.

When I set out in search of what ails Canadian media, I actually didn't expect to discover the degree to which media ownership concentration still beggars belief. It is a very real reason why not just newspapers but all our media are in such disarray. Good journalism tends to break out when there is competition, and there just isn't much of that when everyone's batting for the same team.

And then along comes the Internet and the bottom falls out of your business, and as a newspaper editor you spend the next decade, even longer, steering at an iceberg and (perhaps not unreasonably, given climate change) hoping it will melt before you get there. Except it hasn't, and there's no turning back. Nor should we, because much as *I* love newspapers and I will try to find a way to read one every day till I die, many people don't, and won't.

So is it time to say goodbye to all that? It would be bad news if there were no news, but does the logic hold that it would be bad news if there were no *newspapers*, now that

they are so seldom synonymous with good journalism? Jim
Brown, host of CBC Radio's *The 180*, introduced a guest
on his show in February 2016 by saying that "according to
Paul Watson, a little Darwinism in the media landscape
isn't a bad thing."[10] Watson was interviewed in the wake of
yet another Postmedia contraction in which the company
said it planned to merge a number of big-city newsrooms,
including those of Vancouver's *Sun* and *Province*, so that
one newsroom would produce content for two papers. Watson spent two summers working at the *Vancouver Sun*
in the early 1980s before forging a notable international
career covering some of the world's danger spots (he won
a Pulitzer Prize in 1994 for a photograph of an American
soldier's body being pulled through the streets of Moga-
dishu, Somalia). On *The 180*, he didn't go so far as to call
time on his old newsroom, but Watson said papers like the
Sun are part of "an unhealthy system, and readers are saying it's unhealthy by fleeing in large numbers... there's a
trust deficit, and as people find new sources of information
they're learning what the big ones aren't telling them, and
they don't like that."

That trust deficit, more than anything, seems to por-
tend a rapid end to most Canadian newspapers. "The
media is already well down the list of trusted institutions
and cannot afford to sink further,"[11] writes Madelaine
Drohan, the *Economist's* Canada correspondent and 2015
Prime Ministers of Canada fellow at the Public Policy
Forum. "Canadians aged 15 to 25 have the least confidence

in the media"—they being the coveted millennials who are eventually supposed to take over the country and pay the bills. Without them, my inquiries reveal, like as not there won't be two newspapers left in Vancouver—or in Calgary, Edmonton, or Ottawa—in just a few short years. In some cities, there might not even be one.

Canadian newspapers are basically dead men walking. It is easy to conclude—although hard to accept—that frankly the sooner we stop throwing good money after bad newspapers, the better. The newspaper era is essentially over, even if the need for good journalism has never been greater. Old, slow, and lazy doesn't win the race. It's beyond urgent that we clear the decks and make way for the journalism of tomorrow, because the journalism of today is fast becoming yesterday's news.

ONE

No Country for Old Media:
Our Shrinking Public Square

IT IS PROBABLY fair to say that on any given day, in the hushed halls of power in Canada—on the oaken newspaper racks in our cities' private clubs, in the lobbies of Fairmont hotels, in the offices of Cabinet ministers from coast to coast, on coffee tables in the carpeted confines of our corporate titans—you will be hard-pressed to find a copy of the *Tofino-Ucluelet Westerly News*.

A fatal crash on the Pacific Rim Highway between Tofino and Ucluelet, or a good-news story about the Clayoquot Oyster Festival—"Oyster Fest. shucks locals out of winter's shell"—just won't win many people's attention when thousands of refugees are at the gate, Bombardier is once again at the trough, Rob Ford has breathed his last, and oilman Murray Edwards, shortly after climbing onto a stage with Alberta's NDP premier to vaunt the coming of a carbon tax, has decamped for a more tax-friendly Britain.

Even by the standards of the traditional local rag, the weekly *Westerly News* is a poor excuse for a newspaper. After you've forked out your $1.25, the paper's girth immediately drops by two-thirds when you extract inserts from Home Hardware, No-Frills, Staples, the Brick, and Buy-Low Foods. What's left of the actual newspaper, all 16 pages of it,[1] loses another half to ads. There is one page of amusements (crossword, Sudoku, etc.) and a total of eight stories written by the paper's sole reporter, along with a sprinkling of other stories written by community members whose bylines qualify as "Local Voices." That's it. As for the stories themselves, well, let's just say there are none that would cause even the slightest murmur in the aforementioned chambers of power. Nothing comes remotely close to fulfilling Finley Peter Dunne's oft-cited maxim that good journalism is that which "comforts th' afflicted [and] afflicts th' comfortable."[2]

From sea to shining sea: Journalism's rocky shores

TOFINO AND UCLUELET are hardly alone in being dished up truly execrable fare when it comes to local "news" in Canada. They are two among hundreds of communities across the country that suffer the effects of getting news from one media monopoly or another. The *Westerly News* is one very small link in a chain of "some of the oldest, most trusted community newspapers in North America," if you believe what you read on the website of Black Press, which claims to be the largest independently owned newspaper company in Canada. Its chairman, David (not Conrad) Black, bought his first newspaper in BC, the *Williams Lake Tribune,* in 1975. His company now owns 150 titles in BC, Alberta, Washington state, Hawaii, California, and Ohio.

What "elevates" (their word, not mine) Black Press titles is their "diversity" (ditto); their investment in "grass-roots journalism" (whatever that is) is carried out in "newsrooms with history dating back to the 1800s." If that's a tear of nostalgia threatening to break loose from the corner of your eye, wait till I tell you that, having become rich in inverse proportion to the impoverishment he has wished upon the journalistic quality of dozens of local newspapers across the West, Black also fashions himself as an emerging industrial mogul in the manner of his East Coast concomitants, the good family Irving.

Not content merely to make buckets of money (in 2013, the *Financial Post* estimated Black Press's revenues to be more than half a billion dollars),[3] Black announced in 2012 that he wants to build a multi-billion-dollar oil refinery in Kitimat, a port town in north-central BC that is already home to an Alcan aluminum smelter and a shuttered pulp mill, the town having been built in an era when environmental assets were routinely sacrificed for economic ones. Black correctly predicted that Enbridge's poorly executed

Northern Gateway pipeline project would founder, and certainly the 2015 election of Justin Trudeau's Liberal government seemed to put the last nail in the Northern Gateway coffin when Trudeau vowed to ban tanker traffic of unrefined tar sands fuels from the West Coast.

Black claims his refinery plan is superior because it will ship refined product. He wants to diversify into the oil business because, as he says, "I am for creating thousands of good permanent jobs in BC... billions of new tax dollars for government coffers... reducing the planet's greenhouse gas emissions... building an oil pipeline that will never leak... [and] building a new tanker fleet, owned by a BC company that cannot shirk its liability for a spill at sea, and that carries refined fuels that float and evaporate if spilled."[4] These goals have been freely expressed by Black and dutifully recorded in Kitimat's *Northern Sentinel* newspaper and the nearby *Terrace Standard*, along with other northern papers. Both papers are owned by Black Press.

Although his claim that he can simultaneously refine Alberta bitumen and reduce greenhouse-gas emissions seems preposterous, it remains journalistically unexamined by two of his newspapers, although these papers did note that Black has since changed his mind and now champions rail over pipelines for getting crude to tidewater. "It's safer and way easier," he said.[5] That claim, too, has gone unchallenged in newsrooms, historic or otherwise, populated by Black's "grassroots" journalists.

SWITCH COASTS FOR a moment, and consider the case
of J.D. Irving Limited, the sprawling New Brunswick conglomerate that, unlike David Black's company, started out
in the resource-extraction business and later moved into
newspaper ownership. The Irvings have massive holdings
in just about every walk of Atlantic Canada's industrial
life, and a stranglehold on East Coast journalism that once
attracted the attention (and repelled the recommendations)
of not one but *two* federal commissions of inquiry—the
Davey Report (1970) and the Kent Commission (1981).
The ownership concentration of Irving-owned Brunswick
News was left unimpaired by Senator Keith Davey's rec-
ommendation of passing legislation that would "require the
break-up of regional monopolies, such as that of the Irving
family in New Brunswick, by prohibiting the ownership of
two or more newspapers having 75% or more of the circulation, in one language, in a defined geographical area."[6]
Instead, Brunswick News today has 20 titles big and small,
and boasts that "more than 60% of people in New Brunswick's major cities read one of the publications" owned by
the company.[7] Good for them, you might say, but not so
good for the citizens of New Brunswick, who are notoriously poorly served when it comes to anything approaching
objective reporting about the biggest economic operator
in the province—the owner of all its newspapers. "The
newspapers shy away from covering internal divisions or
leadership issues within the Irving family and companies,"
Bruce Livesey wrote in *Report on Business*,[8] then quoted

Ken Langdon, a former publisher of one of the Irving papers, as saying, "The problem with the Irvings owning the papers is that none of that ever comes out."

New Brunswick, which the Davey Report described as one of two "journalistic disaster areas" at the time (the other was Nova Scotia), was the subject of an episode of Jesse Brown's cage-rattling podcast *Canadaland* in November 2014.[9] "It's like North Korea. It's like the hermit province of New Brunswick," Brown said. His show recounted a pretty thorough litany of all the ills you would expect of a powerful, rich, "notoriously secretive," politically manipulative family monopoly. But it was an exchange from a later *Canadaland* episode that stood out for me. In February 2015, during a live broadcast from St. Thomas University in Fredericton, there was a panel discussion about a local controversy regarding the awarding of timber licences (the Irvings are major landowners, forest harvesters, and lumber millers, among many other things[10]). One of Brown's guests was Green Party MLA David Coon, who had sponsored a bill in the legislature that would have favoured small, independent forest owners and operators. Coon complained that his bill was barely, and poorly, covered by the Irving-owned *Telegraph-Journal*. There is, Coon said, "a chill on the way that people speak about Irving-related businesses or forestry activities that they [Irving companies] are engaged in."[11]

> Coon: It's also not just the way that Brunswick News is covering the stories but also what they're not covering...

Like in BC, the land has never been ceded by the First
Nations in New Brunswick, but you would never know
that was the case or that there were even First Nations in
New Brunswick by reading Brunswick News.

Brown: The [proposed] legislation is directly con-
trary to the interests of the Irvings, and they did cover
it in their paper. Your complaint is that it's on page 5,
it's marginally covered, and the way it's covered charac-
terizes it as something of interest to fringe voices and
nothing to be taken too seriously. Is that accurate?

Coon: Media tends to talk to the powers that be and
tends to reflect the conventional wisdom. If you are not
connected to the powers that be, or if you are not speaking in the narrative or the voice of conventional wisdom,
then you don't tend to have much of a place in the media.

Or much of a place in New Brunswick society at all if
you are an Aboriginal person whose existence, according
to Coon, is effectively unacknowledged by a media monopoly whose owners happen to have a competing interest in
the land and its uses. As for an Aboriginal narrative contributing to the province's conventional wisdom, let alone
being acknowledged as part of Atlantic Canada's traditional wisdom, or Canada's, that evidently is in no danger
of occurring through New Brunswick's conventional media
channels.

In a way, the Black and Irving newspaper oligopolies
serve to rather tidily bracket a Canadian media landscape
that is shockingly out of step with developments occurring

around the world, and that profoundly ill serves Canadians. The West and the East aren't the only places where media concentration exists in Canada (more on that below), but they are arguably where its worst effects manifest themselves in the connection between powerful industrial, natural resource, and other economic interests; those interests' ownership of local media; their subsequent authorship of dominant local, regional, and national narratives; and their overt use of that confluence of interests to comfort themselves and afflict Canadians, *a mari usque ad mare*, with a narrow, self-serving, pro-business (theirs), monocultural view of Canada. If Keith Davey were alive today, he might be heard to utter, *"Plus ça change."*

Newspaper ownership concentration mattered in 1970, when the Davey Report was issued, it mattered in 1981, when the Kent Commission recommended breaking up monopolies, and it matters now. Ownership concentration harms democracy, which thrives on a free press. But "in a country that has allowed so many newspapers to be owned by a few conglomerates, freedom of the press means, in itself, only that enormous influence without responsibility is conferred on a handful of people,"[12] as the Kent Commission concluded 35 years ago. The commission also said flat out that "Industrial conglomerates produce poor newspapers."[13] Twenty-five years later, a Senate report on the state of Canadian media revealed how little things had changed, referring to the Irvings' holdings as an "industrial-media complex."[14]

Dancing with the Devil

CONCENTRATION DOESN'T JUST allow owners and publishers to peddle their impoverished (but self-enriching) views of the world; it also gives rise to brazen political interference. Look at the notorious directive made in October 2015 by Postmedia CEO and president Paul Godfrey that all 16 major newspapers in his stable endorse Stephen Harper's federal Conservatives in their doomed bid to retain power in Ottawa.[15] Even more egregious was what John Barber described in the *Guardian* as "the company's chain-wide blitz supporting Harper [that] culminated a few days before the election when virtually all Postmedia publications replaced their front pages with a pro-Conservative advertisement masquerading as an official notice from Elections Canada, the independent agency managing the vote."[16] This struck many Canadians as a new low for newspaper journalism, or at least for newspaper *publishing*. In fairness, says Margo Goodhand, who was editing the *Edmonton Journal* at the time, "while Godfrey ordered up pro-Tory editorials in all four of his papers in May [during the Alberta provincial election] and across the country federally in October, he was willing to sell any and all front pages to any political party that asked... Because the Tories bought so many front pages that day in the East, it has become some kind of urban legend that Godfrey gave away his papers to the Tories in a political move. Purely fiscal."[17]

Meanwhile, also on the eve of the federal election, the *Globe* revealed the extent to which it has become little more than an oil-soaked rag when it plumped for the Conservatives in its pre-election editorial. Its former editor, John Stackhouse—then recently departed to the hallowed halls of Canadian banking—writes in *Mass Disruption*, a memoir that came out in October 2015, that "editorial boards at major newspapers... [remain] the high church of journalism,"[18] stating that a "well-argued editorial" helps define an organization, by which measure the *Globe* confirmed its status on October 16, 2015,[19] as Canada's village idiot for the day—on arguably the most important day of the year for political journalism save election day itself.

For working journalists, how their paper's owners spend their editorial coin can be utterly demoralizing, and decrees like Godfrey's only illustrate how downright desperate the business prospects are for major newspapers—some would say deservedly so, given the soul-selling behaviour of the Postmedias of the world. "Eight of Canada's daily newspapers disappeared last year," Barber wrote in 2015, "and the leading titles are all operating at [a] loss."[20]

Godfrey's Postmedia already owned the most major city newspapers/web portals in Canada before it earned federal approval in March 2015 to greatly expand its empire by acquiring Quebecor's Sun Media national chain of 173 titles.[21] Postmedia gained its dominance when, backed by a US hedge fund, it acquired much of Canwest's newspaper holdings, which were already saddled with merger debt[22] that had pushed that media conglomerate (TV, print, and digital) into bankruptcy. Since acquiring Canwest's print assets, Postmedia (itself more than $670 million in debt),[23] has bled money and staff[24] while cashing out its real-estate assets. Canada's ever-somnambulant Competition Bureau, at least under Stephen Harper's gimlet-eyed control, saw nothing wrong with the Postmedia/Quebecor transaction,[25] blithely concluding there was no real competition between Postmedia's broadsheets and Sun Media's tabloids, so, by implication, ownership concentration would do no harm. The bureau also said there was an "incentive for the merged company to retain readership and maintain editorial quality in order to continue to attract advertisers to its newspapers," that there was healthy competition "from digital alternatives in an evolving media marketplace," and best of all, there was "existing competition from free local daily newspapers," which, I believe, are those things that people in coloured bibs thrust at commuters when they're struggling to work every morning. That's like saying you really don't need modern medicine because we've still got leeches.

Results that speak volumes

BRAZEN POLITICAL INTERFERENCE? Check. But is ownership concentration the only way to maintain quality and commercial viability in these tough economic times? What would Conrad (not David) Black say? Well, Conrad Black did say this: "Some of [Postmedia's] newspapers have deteriorated a long way from what I remember. Some of it you can't avoid. Some of it you can. But please build the quality. Otherwise, you're going to retreat right into your own end zone, if you'll pardon the sports metaphor."[26] Or continue your death spiral, if you'll pardon a metaphor from the insurance industry. By the time December 2015 came around, the *Globe and Mail's* business section sported a fetching headline: "Postmedia's S&P credit rating is now the same as Greece's."[27] Postmedia had earlier announced plans to cut an estimated $50 million in operating expenses over two years, much of them salaries, but meanwhile had forked out $69 million in interest in its 2015 fiscal year. "A Postmedia spokesperson declined to comment," and honestly, why would they?

Indeed, why say anything in December when you are planning to announce in January another 90 job losses in the chain by merging newsrooms at multiple city newspapers into one each in Vancouver, Calgary, Edmonton, and Ottawa? "We will continue to operate separate brands in each of these markets," Godfrey said in a memo to staff on January 19, 2016. "What is changing is how we produce these products."[28] This, in complete contravention of what he originally told the Competition Bureau, with layoffs to match. And still the debt piles up,[29] with Postmedia "sitting with its own unique time bomb of financial constraints," according to the Canadian Press, and "operating under debt obligations that come due over the next few years at astronomical amounts." Its long-term debt of $25.9 million vaults to $302.7 million in 2017, according to its annual report filed in November 2015. "If Postmedia is unable to repay those debts, or find a solution to refinance what it owes, the company is almost certain to wind up in bank-ruptcy," the CP reported. Second-quarter losses reported in April 2016 totalled $225 million, amid attempts by the company's largest shareholder to get out altogether.[30]

In truth, people living in Vancouver, Edmonton, Cal-gary, and Ottawa—actually in every media market in the country—have been subjected to such insufferably middle-brow journalism for so long now that it's tempting to ask who even cares if Postmedia eventually goes under. Well, the prime minister for one, who tweeted after hearing the company's January announcement that "Journalists are vital to our democracy... I'm saddened to hear of the cuts at #postmedia today and my thoughts are with the affected."[31] The affected, of course, being not just journal-ists but all of us. "Centralized news gathering and opinions, including in local news, do not add to the national debate that helps build a functioning democracy," said Unifor pres-ident Jerry Dias. "With each quieted voice, our democracy suffers."[32] Not so fast, says Kelly Toughill, director of the school of journalism at Nova Scotia's University of King's College, who questions how important newspapers are to democracy when there's so much good content online. "Journalism matters, but the future of newspaper compa-nies should not be confused with the future of journalism,"

Toughill writes. "The demise of newspapers breaks my heart—but it won't break democracy."[33] Chantal Hébert begs to differ, writing in the *Toronto Star* about *La Presse's* almost complete move to digital, save a Saturday print edition, that "the jury is out as to what toll, if any, the shift [to digital] will take on the quality and breadth of [Quebec's] public conversation."[34]

Just think for a moment about what just happened in the preceding passage: informed Canadians debating the importance of newspapers to democracy, a debate waged—democratically—on the editorial pages of *newspapers*. In a Facebook world, where the most that is demanded of readers is that they "like," "love," say "haha" or "wow," be "sad" or "angry," and/or share or comment on a story (and keep it under 20 words or folks will scroll down), it is fair enough to be anxious about the quality and breadth of the public conversation, if it can be considered a conversation at all. That's what's in danger of going missing in Canada if newspapers become extinct.

And then, days later, on January 25, 2016, this: "The *Guelph Mercury*, one of the oldest newspapers in the country, is the latest casualty of a wave of austerity that has swept through Canadian newsrooms this winter."[35] The paper, whose publishing history dates back to Canada's Confederation, published its last print edition four days later. Out on the West Coast, the *Nanaimo Daily News* went dark the same day.[36]

"I'm pretty startled by how quickly things have declined," Dwayne Winseck told the *Globe*.[37] He should know, not only being a Carleton University professor of journalism but a lead researcher for the Canadian Media Concentration Research Project. "Perhaps the most dramatic tale of doom and gloom in the network media economy comes from the experience of newspapers," Winseck wrote, even before the latest round of cuts and closures. "Newspaper revenues drifted downward slowly between 2000 and 2008, but have shrunk immensely since from $5.8 billion to $3.7 billion—a plunge of one-third in half a decade." Of all media in Canada that his study encompasses, newspapers are "the most clear cut case of a medium in decline."[38]

The irony here is that concentration and consolidation have always been seen—at least by owners, and by negligent competition watchdogs—as a justifiable *sine qua non* for media profitability, a bulwark against the vagaries of competition in diminishing markets, a keystone support for keeping the newspaper industry from imploding altogether, taking media diversity down the drain with it. So regulators have tended to approve mega mergers, believing that Canada, with its relatively small, dispersed population, needs to offer corporate media clear pathways to efficiencies so as to retain capacity to do significant journalism—or just survive.[39] In return, as part of the bargain, merging media giants promise to develop and subsidize vital, original Canadian content. However, bottom-line pressures inevitably win out. Today's reality is that concentration and consolidation are simply exacerbating the industry's lack of profitability (Postmedia being essentially now just a debt-service agency for an offshore hedge fund), driving out what little quality journalism is left, but even more damagingly, serving as a huge barrier to the sort of vibrant, variegated media innovation ecosystem, most of it digital, that has begun to flourish elsewhere. Or as John Stackhouse describes it in his book *Mass Disruption,* it is a case of an "innovator's dilemma, the creative deadweight of an old business that not only wouldn't die but kept showing enough signs of life to prevent anyone from trying to break it."[40]

Our so-called "legacy media"—newspapers in particular, but broadcasters, too—are committing a kind of economic and editorial seppuku: they have lost the will to invest in the sort of journalism we used to take for granted, which guts their credibility (and audience), which erodes their revenues, which leads to cutbacks in journalism quality... and so it goes, as Kurt Vonnegut would say. Our legacy media today are too busy servicing debt to adequately serve their public, although to be fair this isn't just a Canadian problem. "Predicting a turnaround in newspapers' fortunes is a loser's bet"[41] wrote the *New York Times'* public editor, Margaret Sullivan, in a column fretting about the threatened state of local investigative reporting. Sullivan said that "with newspaper profits hit hard by the sharp decline in print advertising, and with newsroom staffs withered after endless rounds of cost-cutting layoffs, local investigative journalism is threatened." She cited the American Society of News Editors as saying newspaper staffs in the US have declined by 40 per cent since 2003, thereby "leaving crucial beats vacant and public meetings without coverage... Of course, local newspapers aren't the only places doing local investigative journalism. More and more, nonprofit news organizations, digital start-ups, university-based centers and public radio stations are beginning to fill the gap—sometimes in partnerships. But *they probably won't fully take hold while newspapers, even in their shrunken state, remain the dominant media players in local markets* [emphasis added]."

And there we balance, uncomfortably—our legacy media teetering on the edge of oblivion, and what few upstarts there are tottering along on insufficient capital, their access to revenues blocked by the wounded giants of yore. In "Postmedia-land," former *National Post* and now *Walrus* editor Jonathan Kay says, "The business model has evaporated... Newspapers aren't dead: A generation from now, I believe, the *New York Times* and the *Wall Street Journal* will still be publishing paper editions. And Toronto likely will have a paper, too—likely a single merged upscale product arising from the consolidation of the *National Post, Toronto Star,* and *Globe and Mail.* But the era of the medium-sized, medium-quality daily is in its final act... [a] shrinking newspaper industry means there will be fewer resources available for holding government and business to account—especially when it comes to the big, complicated investigative stories that just can't be done by local broadcast media, or clickbait-oriented web sites."[42]

Say goodbye to those *Gazette*s and *Herald*s and *Citizen*s and *Leader-Post*s, those *StarPhoenix*es, those *Suns* and *Star*s because, Kay says, "the coming media landscape is U-shaped. Which is to say, there will be plenty of mass-produced, ad-financed low-quality content to be found at the cheap, Business Insidery end of the content spectrum. And there also will be people like me and my *Walrus* colleagues creating quality content at the charitably financed top end... In the modern media market, go low, or go high. Hanging out in the middle of the road will put you on the path to corporate extinction."

Hébert contends that print media are "not the only casualty of this ongoing meltdown. Mainstream commercial networks are struggling to adapt to digital viewing habits of their audience—leaving less money to devote to their news coverage. After decades of budget cuts, Radio-Canada and the CBC are shadows of their former selves. So far, the reaction of Canada's political class has mostly ranged from indifference to public hand-wringing. On Twitter... the mayors of the cities involved in the Postmedia announcement expressed regrets at the news. So did Prime Minister Justin Trudeau. But there must be a point when the steady disintegration of our fifth estate's news-gathering and news-getting functions becomes a public policy issue."[43]

The government goes AWOL

THAT POINT HAS surely been reached. It is worth remembering that, in a different age, "Much of the impetus for the creation of the [Kent] commission was the virtually simultaneous closure, on August 26–27, 1980, of two major daily newspapers: the *Ottawa Journal* (owned by the Thomson Corporation) and the *Winnipeg Tribune* (owned by Southam Inc.). These closures gave each chain a monopoly in the two markets, Southam with the *Ottawa Citizen* and Thomson with the *Winnipeg Free Press*."[44] It seems almost quaint, given what has happened since, to think that the closure of two newspapers in two markets could give rise to a national inquiry into the state of the rest of them.

True, Clifford Lincoln has since chaired a two-year House of Commons study of Canadian broadcasting whose 872-page report sank with barely a trace upon its release in 2003.[45] There was also a 2006 Senate inquiry into Canada's media landscape by a committee led by Lise Bacon, which, writes Hébert,

> warned that Canada was tolerating a concentration of media ownership that most other countries would find worrisome. And it noted that the consistent depletion of these resources of the country's public broadcaster compounded the problem.

Some take solace in the notion that Trudeau's government is committed to reinvesting in the CBC. But a

news environment dominated by one media organization—even the public broadcaster—does not amount to
a healthy one.

In any event, what followed the Senate report was
a decade of laissez-faire that often saw owners sympa-
thetic to the government of the day given free rein over
larger media empires, combined with ever-closer-to-the-
bone cuts to the CBC.

What we have today is a weaker public broadcaster in
a field of journalistic ruins and Canada's national fabric
is the poorer for it.[46]

In early 2016, Liberal MP Hedy Fry declared that she
would try her hand at heading a Commons committee to
study "how Canadians, and especially local communities,
are informed about local and regional experiences through
news, broadcasting, digital and print media… The thing
about politics is that the time comes one day when stuff is
facing you so hard that you have to do something about it.
That time has come."[47] Of course, for successive Canadian
government media inquiries spanning more than 35 years
now, "doing something about it" has meant studying it.
The record of action resulting from those studies brings to
mind Kitty Muggeridge's famously delaminating comment
about British media star David Frost, whom she dismissed
50 years ago as having "risen without a trace."[48] So too our
governments' interest in the state of our media, and our
newspapers in particular.

In a follow-up column to her *New York Times* lament for the future of investigative journalism, Margaret Sullivan wrote that while "digital-era economics have devastated newspaper staffs,"[49] digital platforms like ProPublica have come to fill some of the space vacated by local media. She interviewed Richard Tofel, president of ProPublica, which has emerged as the early gold standard for how a loss of ink doesn't have to mean a lack of stink (as in creating one, like any good news organization should). While understandably bullish about his own organization, Tofel told Sullivan that investigative journalism's transition online won't be a smooth one. With newspapers still dominant in many cities, he said there's not enough of a gap to create great need for new players, funded in new ways, including through philanthropy. "Mr. Tofel told [Sullivan], 'There's still an irrational amount of print advertising' supporting newspaper economics. 'But the next recession will be very unkind to newspapers.' By the time it's over [Tofel said], 'seven-day-a-week newspapers will be the exception, not the rule.'"

In this area alone, it seems, Canada is fast becoming a world leader, our (relatively) paper-less future approaching much more quickly than we think. In August 2015, the Poynter Institute, one of the most respected journalism schools in the US, reported that Canadian media are failing at a rate that is as worrying as it is seemingly inevitable. Poynter cited Ken Goldstein, a leading media business analyst, who predicts, "In 2025, it is likely that there will be few, if any, printed daily newspapers" in Canada and "there might be no local broadcast stations" in our country just 10 years from now.[50] (Note that this was before closures and cuts announced towards the end of 2015 and in early 2016.)

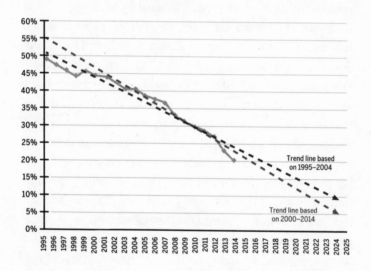

FIGURE 2. Total daily newspaper paid circulation as a percentage of households, Canada, 1995–2014, with trend lines to 2025. (Communications Management Inc.; appeared on Poynter.org)

Figure 2 illustrates the severity of the challenge to mainstream newspapers by charting the decline in paid newspaper circulation, which as a percentage of Canadian households has fallen from just under 50 per cent in 1995 to 20 per cent in 2014. If those declines continue, circulation will amount to only 5 to 10 per cent of households in

2025—too little, Goldstein says, "to support a viable print business model for most general interest daily newspapers." As for television, Goldstein says the Canadian broadcast sector has failed to adapt as the traditional over-the-air model has given way to cable and Internet delivery. In the US, huge political advertising revenue windfalls and retransmission fees keep local stations successful financially. Canada lacks those market factors, and Goldstein says local stations have become "a much less profitable business—and now [find themselves] in a money-losing situation."

Meanwhile, government support for public broadcasting in Canada was drastically undercut by the Harper government, and the 2015 election campaign provided further illustration of how poorly served the country is by innovative and independent media. This was especially true at the local level, where many mid-sized markets now have no local newspaper or broadcaster.

Like concentration, the outright elimination of media voices matters. In the US, there is a tradition of philanthropic support for and investment in journalism and media innovation—think the Pew Charitable Trusts, the Knight Foundation, and the Nieman Foundation, among many others. In the UK, the Scott Trust exists to support the groundbreaking and fiercely independent work of the *Guardian*. In Europe, there is some support for digital media innovation. In Canada, there is negligible philanthropic or state support for journalism of any kind at a time when we need it most—when our public institutions are failing to address many serious, intractable social and economic issues; when our governments have become increasingly secretive and bureaucrats have been muzzled; when advocacy in the philanthropic sector has essentially been outlawed; and when young people in particular, and indigenous people most of all, are disengaged and disinterested in political processes that have marginalized them or ignored them altogether.

The election of the Trudeau Liberals in October 2015 might alleviate some of the more glaring attacks on civil society that were a hallmark of Harperism, but political cycles are short, and politicians are notoriously ill-equipped to keep their promises. And there are plenty of provincial and municipal (and Aboriginal) governments and agencies that don't come with quite the Camelot appeal of Trudeau's—they, as much if not more than the federal government, need the constant attention of good reporting, but where is it going to come from? As Ken Goldstein asks, "If the two largest sources of spending on journalism [newspapers and broadcasters] in Canada today might be gone or much diminished in 2025, what will take their place?" Support for journalism and emerging media business models should have "high priority as a... concern of public and private policy."[51]

In his mandate letter[52] to Heritage Minister Mélanie Joly, the prime minister did the obvious thing, which was to ask her to restore funding to the CBC and increase funding to Telefilm Canada and the National Film Board, among other things. The freshly minted government seemed to have been caught unawares by the collapse of a Canadian industry that, were it the auto sector, let alone the energy sector, would have provoked vastly more gnashing of teeth and delegations to the Hill. The closest Trudeau came to giving Joly a licence to do something about private-sector media was an instruction to "work with the Minister of Infrastructure and Communities to make significant new investments in cultural infrastructure as part of our investment in social infrastructure." Do our media qualify as social infrastructure? Surely they are as important as clean water, good transit, and a sustainable energy grid. Encouragingly, Joly stepped up after six months on the job—"I'm a heritage minister who thinks about digital technology first and foremost—that's how I consume information and music. I'm a product of my generation"[53]—and announced a sweeping review of Canada's broadcasting, media, and cultural industries, a welcome leap beyond the modest mandate prescribed by Trudeau.

The "Cancon review" can't come soon enough. At a moment of flowering global digital potential, you might expect our media landscape to be quickly diversifying, full of competing models, new approaches, and strong viewpoints, rich with choices for an information-hungry citizenry. Yet left to the private sector, Canada has been stuck in a decade-old holding pattern, its corporate media ownership among the Western world's most highly concentrated, and most new digital experiments in actual "grassroots" or independent journalism are doomed to fail because they are under-capitalized and toil mostly undiscovered by readers or subscribers. Elsewhere in the world, the Internet's deep erosion of print and broadcast ad revenues has provoked a bright, diverse, if somewhat volatile response in the digital realm. In Canada, by contrast, independent alternatives remain relatively few. Canada is frankly missing out on the next, great media revolution, and that holds back our ability to champion innovation and contribute to sense making and solution finding as participants in our political, social, economic, and cultural discourse.

There's no doubt the advent of the new Liberal government in Ottawa in 2015 heralded a long-overdue assaying of the nation's condition—and some immediate, creative responses to it. Right off the bat, the government opened the shutters on what our scientists are discovering, what our statisticians are measuring, what our federal ministers are charged with doing, and what government members are allowed to say—and not just to the media. It also promised to revise, in favour of increased transparency, federal practice with respect to access to information. In addition, Ottawa's willingness to plump for a 1.5-degree warming limit in Paris and insistence on language that affirms the primacy of indigenous rights in the face of energy developments; its promise to welcome Syrian refugees enthusiastically; to nix tanker traffic off the West Coast; to champion an inquiry into missing and murdered Aboriginal women; to lead by example with a gender-balanced cabinet; to invest in urban infrastructure—all these decisions were a gesture towards a Canada arguably more at one with itself.

Under Joly's guidance, the Liberals seem ready to extend their reformist zeal into the country's media landscape, and it is critically important they get it right if they are serious about engaging in a national conversation about how to tackle our challenges. If the government is sincere about encouraging our so-called civil society to press its advantage in a newly receptive federal capital, if it wants thinking Canadians to have access to better newspapers, to see better television, to listen to better radio, and to find something better than clickbait on their tablets and phones—well, all that is a function of how rich, diverse, and accessible the media infrastructure is that enables local, regional, and national conversations to take place. A government with a new-found curiosity about the state of Canadian media doesn't need to invoke its power to command witnesses to quickly discover the troubling contours in Canada's current media landscape. Canada's journalism is in ruins, and our nation is the poorer for it. Just look around.

In addition to the reduction of newspapers into a highly concentrated, nutrient-free, quivering intellectual Jell-O, ownership of newer "platform media"—that is, the modern-day providers of wired, wireless, Internet, cable, satellite, and Internet protocol television (IPTV)—is also, according to the Canadian Media Concentration Research Project's Dwayne Winseck, "highly concentrated or at the high-end of the moderately concentrated scale."[54] And even if newspaper and magazine ownership concentration is past its historical peak, "this needs to be set against two other realities: first, both industries have fallen on hard times, newspapers more so than magazines, and as the big players stumble, they are losing market share and, in some cases, they are being broken up, with significant divestitures leading to the emergence of a stronger second tier of newspaper publishers: e.g. Transcontinental, Glacier and Black Press, notably."[55]

In other words, the decline of our legacy media hasn't had any upside in terms of loosening up media ownership, but rather has caused the baton of Canadian newspaper ownership concentration to pass to smaller chains, to the Blacks and Irvings and their ignominious ilk. Meanwhile, for the 80 per cent of Canadians who now lead urban, not rural, lives, media concentration is equally alive and well wherever they look. Four giants—Shaw/Corus, Quebecor, Bell, and Rogers—own most of Canada's TV news broadcast media.[56]

As for the national arena, in addition to public and private broadcasters, we are home to two self-declared national newspapers. Even Toronto isn't spared the presence of Postmedia, which owns the increasingly callow *National Post*. The other self-styled national newspaper, of course, is the *Globe and Mail*—soon to inhabit the upper floors of a 17-storey office tower on King Street East, which, we are told by publisher Phillip Crawley, is a "sign of faith in the future."[57] And why not? It will be situated, as any self-respecting *Globe* subscriber in Toronto would know, a mere block away from Downtown Porsche, which nicely dovetails with the *Globe's* desired target audience. "We are really only interested in readers who earn more than $100,000," Crawley told the World Publishing Expo in 2013.[58] In his search for a "high-end market," Crawley is apparently happy to target just 1 Canadian in 20, which doesn't really make the *Globe* a national newspaper at all, does it? At least not until we all start driving Porsches.

Stop *La Presse!*

IN MONTREAL, WHAT is perhaps Canada's most far-reaching experiment in a digital make-over of a legacy newspaper has been taking place at *La Presse*. To recall Margaret Sullivan's earlier point that digital innovation will find it tough going when legacy newspapers remain in place, *La Presse* is the only large newspaper in Canada thus far to essentially close up shop as a paper after investing in a tablet version of itself, called *La Presse*+. To pull that off, in 2011 the paper "boosted its staffing significantly as part of a $40-million investment to launch and develop *La Presse*+."[59] That employment gain proved to be more of a dead cat bounce, really, as *La Presse* eventually made good on its vow to discontinue publishing a printed weekday edition, at the cost of 102 permanent and 56 temporary jobs. As the paper's president and publisher, Guy Crevier, told employees in September 2015, "We're no longer the newspaper that's existed for 131 years. We're a new company with a new model."[60]

Even before the ink had dried at *La Presse*, its *La Presse+* tablet model caught the eye of the *Toronto Star*, which paid a mint for the Quebec publisher's intellectual property and hired "dozens of new editorial staff"[61] to tool up its own tablet edition, *Star Touch*, in September 2015. Perhaps even more than the tablet experiment in Montreal, many eyes fell on Toronto (the fourth-largest media market in North America) because it is English speaking and the *Star* claimed its tablet foray would not come at the expense of its print edition. Maybe more of *its* new jobs would stick? By November 2015, the *Star* was boasting in excess of 100,000 downloads of its new app,[62] although it was also forced to rename the app *Toronto Star Touch*, reportedly because people didn't understand it was a *Toronto Star* product— they could be forgiven for having thought it was a porn site. Anyway, one step forward, three steps back. Postmedia had beaten Torstar to the punch with evening tablet editions launched in 2014 as part of what it labelled its Reimagined venture into digital innovation. But after about 18 months, Postmedia "quietly discontinued the evening tablet editions for its 'Reimagined' products in Ottawa, Montreal and Calgary, citing a lack of reader and advertiser support."[63]

This, around the same time that *Star Touch* reached its first digital milestone of 100,000 downloads. So which of our legacy media titans, wrestling to come up with a life-saving digital strategy, was getting it right? Well, neither of them.

"What is it with Canada and tablets?" asked Joshua Benton, director of the Nieman Journalism Lab at Harvard University, during a *Canadaland* panel discussion in January 2016.[64] US publishers went down that path years ago after the initial flush of enthusiasm for the iPad, Benton said, but got over it fast. "No one got the audience they were looking for. Everybody shut things down. Everybody realized they had lost a few years by putting all this energy into the tablet when they should have put it into the smart phone." Madelaine Drohan, in her paper for the Public Policy Forum, quotes Patrick McGuire of VICE Canada as saying, "Star Touch is my favourite example of people not getting it."[65] Paul Godfrey seemed to delight in Torstar's misguided investment in digital. "They're way off base and they spent a fortune," he said. "Our philosophy here is fail fast. I don't think they recognize that… everybody's got to experiment, but they keep spending and spending like crazy on it."[66] Although a little less crazily as 2016 dawned with the news that the *Star* had laid off 10 members of its tablet team.[67] By March, Torstar had revealed that "just 65,000 tablets are opening Star Touch each week," which was, according to CEO and president David Holland, "slower than we'd anticipated."[68] Later that month, publisher John Cruickshank, principal author of the *Star*'s tilt towards tablets, resigned.[69]

Cruickshank's dignified departure came after months of caterwauling between Torstar and Postmedia that started in the festive season of 2015 and treated media watchers to a less than salutary, mostly unedifying exchange that was long on bluster and short on anything that would give readers, and perhaps more importantly investors, any signal that either company had a sensible plan for the future. If you were to write a tabloid headline about the pissing match between Torstar and Postmedia, it would probably appear in print as "*Star* bites *Post* bites *Star*"—which would be funny, if it were not so sad.

Torstar chair John Honderich opened hostilities by rather airily taking Godfrey to task for his "dramatic order" that Postmedia titles endorse Stephen Harper: "Surely those in Postmedia communities deserved far, far better."[70] Honderich doubled down a couple of months later, accusing Godfrey of "trifling with the truth about the newspaper industry"[71] by claiming Postmedia had no choice but to seek offshore investment for its Canwest acquisition because no Canadian media company had bid on those assets. Torstar had made just such a bid, Honderich recalled, but "The New York hedge funds, with Godfrey as their front, eventually won the day." All this was too much for Post-media's resident pit bull, Terence Corcoran, the *National Post*'s bilious business columnist, who tripled down when he took three pages in a February 2016 edition of the *Post* to bemoan what he called "a concerted effort to malign and destroy the reputation" of Postmedia by Honderich.[72] Corcoran's own takedown accused Honderich of presiding over a "Torstar shareholder bonfire... with the company's stock price tumbling again to hit an all-time low $2.11 on Jan. 24," implying that Honderich's column about Godfrey trifling with the truth about the industry was intended to divert Torstar investors' gaze from Torstar's plummeting stock price.

Soon after, the *Star* called Postmedia a "cancer on Canadian journalism,"[73] something Corcoran didn't take kindly to either. He accused the author of that story, David Olive, of "channelling Honderich's brain waves" when Olive called Godfrey's claims to have rescued the Canwest newspaper chain "a lie." Olive had claimed Postmedia was paying hundreds of millions to "quick-buck" US hedge funds that were poised to raid it and make off with all the assets: Postmedia "has erased about $503 million in shareholder value, a record in the 264-year history of Canadian newspapers." Corcoran responded, "That, as Olive might say, is a lie. It is certainly not true. There was no mention in Olive's story of the steady decline in Torstar's revenues—or its collapsing shareholder value. Since 2004, Torstar's shareholder value has dropped from a peak of $30.60 a share, or $1.9 billion, to $2 today, about $175 million. In other words, Torstar has erased $1.7 billion in shareholder value since 2004, making Torstar—and not Postmedia—guilty of the largest destruction of value in the 264-year history of

Canadian newspapers. The Torstar value decline is three times greater than that of Postmedia."

What is fascinating about this rhetorical clash of the clans, more befitting last century's Fleet Street chest beaters like Lord Beaverbrook or Robert Maxwell than our typically more muted Canadian media moguls, is that both sides are right: both Torstar and Postmedia, once cash cows, have stopped producing milk. Corcoran actually put it well when he wrote, "What this war is about may be reduced to a simple question: Which of the major newspaper companies will hit the wall first, and which is most likely to survive? This could be the last battle for the *Star*, a company that, in one form or another, has never been able to lift itself out of its Toronto home." But surely the same sword hanging over Torstar cuts the air above the head of Postmedia too, and it's hard to argue with Olive's conclusion that, "Postmedia is giving private ownership of an essential public service a bad name. Its charade of pretending to operate its papers in the public interest cannot end soon enough."

Listening to these death rattles from two of the big newspaper publishers left in Canada—or small ones, if asset value is the measuring stick—it's hard to conclude with any confidence that either can last long, or that either will leave much behind. Jonathan Kay, as previously mentioned, talked of there one day being in Toronto some sort of "upscale product arising from the consolidation of the *National Post*, *Toronto Star*, and *Globe and Mail*."[74]

Don't count on it. More likely is that the *Globe* will survive, and it will have little incentive to invest in better journalism until new and better competition comes along.

That competition will undoubtedly be digital, if and when the search for some kind of online elixir finds its mark. But for now, mark the date—December 31, 2015—when *La Presse* printed its last weekday newspaper and went all in on digital.[75] We may yet look back on that date as a red-letter day for Canadian journalism, because unlike with the *Guelph Mercury* and others like it, at least in *La Presse*'s case, its closure was planned and a digital doppelgänger had been readied to take its place. Note that the tablet didn't add any more journalistic capacity—in fact, when the dust settled, there were four fewer staff when *La Presse* went digital in 2015 than back in 2011,[76] when it made the decision to take that route. *La Presse*'s adventure, if it provides any guidance at all, seems to suggest that the best a newspaper can hope for from such an exercise is to staunch an outflow that at times has felt like a flood. Understandably, the union that represents newsroom staff at *La Presse* isn't convinced management got it right. "It was a lot more [cuts] than what we expected, and we're really worried about *La Presse*'s capacity to publish its edition every day with the staff level that [was announced]," said Charles Côté, president of le Syndicat des travailleurs de l'information de La Presse (STIP) and the paper's environment reporter. "I'm not sure we're going to be able to maintain the high level of quality that we have right now."[77]

Looking for the Q spot

I'M SORRY, DID somebody say the word *quality*? Over in the broadcast world, another example of loss of quality and capacity, not to mention diminished diversity, came in May 2015 when Rogers closed down news broadcasts by its multicultural broadcaster, Omni, to save $5 million.[78] In cutting 110 positions from its broadcast operations, it promised, ominously, to "[transform] the daily newscasts of its multicultural Omni stations into current affairs shows that will spend more air time on each story but won't include original reporting." Jinny Sims, at the time an NDP Member of Parliament for Newton–North Delta, in BC, said the move was damaging for the large Punjabi-speaking population in her riding. "To get the news and its nuances in your own language makes a huge, huge differ-ence for you to be able to participate in a democracy and in our society."

All of Canada's biggest news media corporations have severely downsized their staff over the past several years, trimming about 10,000 journalists between 2008 and 2013 alone, according to Jan Wong[79]—a trend that has continued and shows no signs of abating, judging by a cat-alogue of cuts maintained by Montreal-based freelancer Steve Faguy, whose last blog post in 2015 was a requiem for Hamilton, Ontario's, CHCH, which Faguy considered "Canada's last best hope for the idea of truly local television. It failed." Seventy-one full-time and 15 part-time positions were lost.[80] Mind you, the low-water mark in 2015 for television was probably hit one month earlier, in November, when Bell Media announced dramatic cuts to its television stable, shedding 270 jobs in Toronto and 110 jobs in Montreal,[81] plus cuts in other regions. "This is likely just the start of a radical downsizing in mainstream Canadian TV,"[82] wrote the *Globe*'s television critic John Doyle. "What Bell Media did will very likely be done, eventually, by Rogers and Shaw." (Actually, Rogers Media took another whack in January 2016, when it cut another 200 jobs from its television, radio, and publishing divisions.)[83] Doyle went on to rather succinctly conclude that, "Canadian TV is screwed. For now." Doyle believes that television will be saved—even in the fast-approaching era of "cord-cutters" and "cord-nevers," and cheaper "pick-and-pay" options for TV subscribers who choose to stay with cable and satellite television: "There's no doubt in my mind the Canadian TV racket will recover, after a long and brutal battering. Profits will never reach the ecstatic levels of the past and fewer people will get rich, but Canadian TV will remain what is, essentially: a protected business arena... There is a hunger for it... television is the defining storytelling medium of this century." Doyle may yet find himself satiating his hunger by eating those words.

NATURALLY, FEWER JOURNALISTS results in thinner coverage—and much less in-depth public-interest journalism, the kind that's the costliest to produce and the riskiest to publish. Increasingly anemic bottom lines have caused publishers to blur the once-sharp line between journalism and paid advertising.[84] Today's hot new trend is "native advertising"[85]—news media helping paying clients develop artificial news stories (rather than display ads) and placing them amidst their own news stories with small-font disclaimers. Postmedia, the *Globe and Mail*, and the *Toronto Star* have all loudly launched such new services. Key to native advertising's appeal is its placement[86]—directly within traditional editorial areas of the papers. Where this self-cannibalizing of news organizations' credibility can lead is illustrated by Postmedia's presentation[87] to the Canadian Association of Petroleum Producers, promising that "Postmedia and CAPP will bring energy to the forefront of our national conversation" with "topics to be directed by CAPP and written by Postmedia"—including 12 single-page "Joint Ventures" in the *National Post*, as well as 12 major newspapers including the *Vancouver Sun,* the *Calgary Herald*, and Victoria's *Times-Colonist*. It's hard to imagine journalistic standards sinking much lower, although that is a thought best served hold. This is how Madelaine Drohan describes it: "There has always been a dance between editors and advertisers: only now it is more intimate, says Marie-Claude Ducas, who writes about media for *Le Journal de Montréal*. 'Carole Beaulieu, the editor and publisher of *L'actualité*, says it used to be like a line dance, but now it is a tango, making it easier to step on each other's toes.'"[88]

One other development that has lowered editorial standards has been the contracting out of various newspaper functions, not just reporting, that used to take place on-site in actual newsrooms. As Jan Wong noted in 2013, "Whole departments have been outsourced, including that of copyediting and layout. For instance, Postmedia... moved much of its editorial production to a centralized location in Hamilton, Ont. To cut costs, the *Toronto Star*, the country's largest newspaper, and the *Globe and Mail*, have shifted editing and page-design work to an outside company, Pagemasters North America. Both the *Star* and the *Globe* own stakes in Pagemasters through the Canadian Press. At Pagemasters, the top union rate for an editor is $48,000, compared to about $85,000 at the *Star*."[89]

Anyone who has ever worked in a real newsroom has experienced a love-hate relationship with city desk, from which editors assign local stories, and the "rim," where copy editors cast their jaundiced but experienced eyes over raw copy and, in the view of most reporters, savage their lustrous prose. This copy-editing isn't just about catching typos or shortening a windy story—it is also about bringing the accumulated wisdom of a newsroom to bear in a way that recognizes local culture, geography, history, personalities, and idiosyncrasies. Maureen Dowd, in a column I read several years ago[90] and that haunts me still, told the story of *Pasadena Now*, whose editor, James Macpherson, was referred to as a pioneer of "glocal" news. "Where can I get people who can write the word for less?" Dowd described him as thinking, and the answer to his question turned out to be India. He fired his seven staff members in Pasadena and assigned coverage of local issues to six freelancers in India, who wrote news and features using telephones, email, press releases, web harvesting, and live video streaming from a cellphone at Pasadena's city hall. Macpherson paid per piece, just like the garment industry, and he didn't pay very much: $7.50 for 1,000 words. As for journalistic standards? One of the "reporters" told Dowd by email that, "I try to do my best, which need not necessarily be correct always." For instance, "Regarding Rose Bowl, my first thought was it was related to some food event but then found that is related to Sports field." Note to the editor: the word *sports* in the preceding sentence should be lower case, but then who you gonna call to fix that? Oh right, Pagemasters.

Meanwhile, from China comes news that "a robot called Dreamweaver wrote a flawless, 916-word financial report in one minute."[91] That should send a shiver down the spine of whichever journalists are left who still have one.

AND THEN THERE'S the "Mother Corp," the final stop on our tour of Canadian media in distress. The CBC has long been thought of as a safe harbour from the tendency of corporate media to bow to the biases of advertisers, and to locate only where news businesses can turn a profit. However, the publicly funded model is under severe stress as resources dwindle, and even as they are restored, internal debate roils about our public broadcaster's priorities.

On the resources side, in mid-2014 CBC brass said they were looking to cut as much as 25 per cent of the broadcaster's workforce over five years[92] to respond to a $130-million funding cut inflicted by the Harper Conservatives. Many of those cuts, said CBC executives, would be to television and radio, thanks to the shift to mobile-device content and an "even more local" focus. One of the most controversial decisions was to put the CBC's in-house documentary unit on the chopping block. Linden MacIntyre, then recently retired from *The Fifth Estate*, co-signed a letter to CBC president Hubert Lacroix saying, "CBC Television, to be true to its core mandate, needs more long-form journalism and legacy programming—not less."[93] In response to management's claims that it could source more documentaries from independent producers (who already accounted for 75 per cent of docs aired by the CBC), MacIntyre insisted that the CBC has more power to do "fearless journalism" than independents because legal and financial pressures make independents more risk-averse. "The DNA of Canadian documentary production has to be preserved in an institutional setting, because that's where chances get taken, that's where innovation happens, that's where controversy is embraced—and if we lose that we'll never get it back," MacIntyre said.

Former CBC executive Alain Saulnier accused Lacroix of "collaborating in what I would call the great dismantling of the public broadcaster in collusion with the political powers that be... All developed western democracies recognize the need for an independent public service broadcaster. Most fund it properly. We are now at the third-lowest level of public funding among all OECD countries—and this for a country of immense geography and complex diversity with two official languages and many more aboriginal ones."[94] MacIntyre and Saulnier's critiques, and many more, invite the question of whether the CBC is retreating from its vital and distinctive role, on television and radio, as a facilitator of our national conversation—and whether money is really the problem.

The federal Liberals have pledged to restore up to $150 million in cuts to the CBC and Radio-Canada imposed by Harper, who "made no effort to hide his disdain for a public broadcaster he considered largely a waste of taxpayer money, entrenched in its liberal bias and increasingly irrelevant as a cultural arbiter," Konrad Yakabuski wrote in the *Globe*.[95] Yakabuski professes doubt that any but "a small minority of Canadians, those for whom the public broadcaster is either a religion or source of income," have noticed anything different in the wake of funding cuts...

> which raises questions about why it needs an extra $150-million. To restore supper-hour local newscasts to 90 minutes, when the CBC has long been a local news ratings laggard whose lunch is eaten by CTV affiliates and other private stations? To reinstate an in-house documentary unit, when the latter had long ago ceased producing distinctive and noteworthy content such as *Canada: A People's History*? To hire more celebrity

hosts so that its public affairs programming gets even
more personality-driven and similar to that of private broadcasters? To imitate private networks with
more mediocre dramas and sitcoms that purport to tell
Canadian stories but to which Canadians demonstrate
their indifference by leaving the CBC with a 6-per-cent
prime-time market share?

John Doyle, meanwhile, says that "while CBC is in a better relationship with this government, it is not necessarily
in the best phase of its relationship with the paying public.
Even CBC's strongest supporters cannot turn a blind eye
to the narrative of the last two years—Peter Mansbridge's
and Rex Murphy's paid speaking engagements, the [Jian]
Ghomeshi scandal, the Amanda Lang debacle and the
strange and sudden departure of Evan Solomon. That's a
lot."[96]

Sure, the CBC needs money, but it also needs what
Doyle calls "a dose of common sense and it needs a
reminder that, while it's a special service, it cannot be
remote from the principle that it is indeed a service." A service, indeed. A cultural arbiter, ideally. And one that, while
it is funded by government, needs to operate completely
free of government interference in order to uphold one of
the tenets of its journalistic guidelines, that "public interest
guides all our decisions."[97]

Just as important as money is a philosophical reinvest-
ment in the purpose of the CBC. Its governance "urgently

needs reform, in the public interest," says Alain Saulnier,[98] and somehow the headlock that Parliament has over the CBC's budget allocations needs to be broken. Saulnier dates the erosion of the CBC's independence back to 1968, when Trudeau (Pierre, not Justin) began to attack the CBC's budget because of political coverage that he deemed too separatist. Jean Chrétien lashed out at the CBC in 1995 after the Quebec referendum. Harper hastened the rot when he appointed to the CBC board "those who contribute financially to the Conservative party," according to Saulnier. Justin (not Pierre) Trudeau should encourage Heritage Minister Mélanie Joly in her review to focus less on topping up the CBC's budget and more on transforming the corporation from what it has become—an outdated, tone-deaf, ponderous, and slow-witted kind of Canadian Borecasting Corporation—into a facilitator of a deep and enduring conversation that this country needs to have with itself. That conversation should be based not on news cycles that others are better at chasing, but is one that should take place every day of the year in places—topical and geographical—that other media cannot or will not reach.

The Joly review began in the spring of 2016 with an on-line poll asking Canadians, "What are the key roles for CBC/Radio-Canada to play in supporting Canadian content creation, discovery and export in a digital world?"[99] Respondents are asked to select up to five items from the following:

- Making sure all Canadians have access to content across platforms of their choice, particularly digital platforms
- Providing local content
- Reflecting the diversity of Canadian culture and communities
- Providing quality news and information programming
- Engaging audiences in democratic debate
- Being an incubator for Canadian creative talent and training the next generation of content creators
- Striking partnerships with other players, including other public broadcasters, to extend content to new audiences at home and abroad
- Providing services to official-language minority communities
- Providing services to Canada's Indigenous peoples

To which I hope participants answer, "All of the above." Bottom line: the CBC needs to become a service again—an essential, trusted part of our national infrastructure, just like newspapers used to be. And if it is seen as such and can be trusted to deliver innovative and truly differentiated content and capacity that is beyond the purview or the free-market inclinations of private broadcasters, then maybe a case can be made to fully subsidize the CBC. "You could imagine a sharp split in which the public broadcasters are fully subsidized and fully Canadian and prevented from selling advertising, and the privately owned TV networks are relieved of their Cancon obligations and free to seek foreign investment," Simon Houpt wrote in the *Globe*.[100] Certainly I can imagine a CBC that, like Britain's BBC and Australia's ABC, is wholly government-funded. The sooner Canada's national broadcaster sheds its schizophrenic funding model, thenceforth owing a duty of service solely to Canada's citizens and not to commercial interests, the better.

TWO

What's Happening Across the Pond?

A T FIRST GLANCE, it might not seem axiomatic that unearthing solutions to what ails Canadian journalism might be aided by tilling the vinous hillsides of Umbria, but in April 2015 I took myself to the Etruscan city of Perugia for just that purpose. This was the start of an *enquête* that also took me to London, Boston, New York, and Sydney, Australia, in search of clues about who's getting journalism right in the 21st century, or at least is confronting the challenges rather than shirking them. Perugia has been host for the past decade to the multiple offerings of the International Journalism Festival. I partook of the IJF's ninth edition, in 2015, where more than 650 speakers in 250 separate events plumbed just about every topic in world journalism you could think of (and a few you simply wouldn't). Some of the proceedings are captured in a magazine produced by festival organizers.[1] My own take-aways appear below. Unless otherwise noted, these findings stem from my notes from festival sessions, or in situ interviews with various speakers and participants. Some of this material was previously published in the *Tyee*.[2]

What I heard:

1. Technology is king.
2. Legacy media are dying.
3. New media are cropping up all over, and no one knows what will survive or how.
4. Journalism has, in many ways, never been so important now that the world is awash in data.
5. There is hope.

It is abundantly clear that "legacy media" institutions, such as newspapers and "destination" television news shows, have all but lost the battle for audience as "digital natives" come of age and want everything in the palm of their hand, literally. Canadian media consultant Dan Dunsky, in an essay in *Medium*, cites estimates that "at some point this year [2016], there will be 2 billion smartphones in use globally. By 2020, that number is projected to rise to 6 billion. When these phones are connected to the internet, they make everyone a source of information—free to tell the stories they want, free to describe things as they see them, free from someone else making these decisions for them."[3] There is simply no going back. This has enormous implications for journalism as a business and a vocation, but most importantly as a bearer of critical information and shaper of formative insights to guide public discourse and decision-making.

The issue is not one of demand. According to the evidence advanced in Perugia, the public's appetite for news and information is as insatiable as ever. As for supply, if you consider the sheer *volume* of information that's at hand, there is plenty of that to go around. (Dunsky cites IBM as saying that every day, we create 2.5 quintillion bytes of data. I'm not sure what a quintillion even is, but it sounds like a lot.)

It isn't so much an issue of quantity as one of the quality of the content and the nature of its dissemination. The disruption to legacy media caused by the eruption of the Internet is driving phenomenal innovation in the digital realm, and some of this might actually have positive consequences for audience engagement.

Admittedly, it is hard to be terribly sanguine about the triumphalism exhibited by the likes of Google and Facebook—who between them, in Canada at least, are gobbling up two-thirds of our Internet advertising revenues—along with Twitter, which has more than 320 million registered users, a seething mass of content providers "updating the world" with an incandescent barrage of information. There was much debate in Perugia about the merits of "social"— it is apparently passé to use the expression "social media." Clearly, the vacuity of much of what is transmitted via social—all that clickbait and, of course, all those cat pictures—disqualifies much of it as journalism, but social does have its place, especially in regions and among populations where real journalism doesn't exist or is discouraged by the state. (By the time the 10th International Journalism Festival convened, in April 2016, Facebook, Google, Apple, Twitter, and even Spotify had dived into full-throated news distribution of their own. Facebook had made its Instant Articles "open to all publishers—of any size, anywhere in the world."[4] Google's Accelerated Mobile Pages project[5] similarly "is an open source initiative that embodies the vision that publishers can create mobile optimized content once and have it load instantly everywhere.")

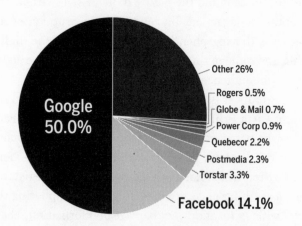

FIGURE 3. Who gets the advertising revenue in Canada? (Canadian Media Concentration Research Project; appeared in "Does serious journalism have a future in Canada?" by Madelaine Drohan)

Cracking the code

THE WIDESPREAD CONSENSUS at Perugia 9.0 was that technology, and what it enables, is now the biggest factor in world journalism, and that technology's *sine qua non*, data, now rules. Data-driven journalism, according to John Crowley, digital editor of the *Wall Street Journal*, is creating "completely different newsroom forms" and is changing the definition of what a journalist is. "Some of the best work we do is in purely graphical form," said Aron Pilhofer, formerly of the *New York Times* and now executive editor of digital at the *Guardian*. One consequence of all this, Crowley said, is that the single biggest log-jam in the development of modern newsrooms is not a lack of talented people writing great stories, but of talented people writing great code.

But if the coders are in charge, then what, in the end, will we actually be *reading* and *writing*? And will we even be reading at all, or merely watching? (Or playing! The BBC has come under fire for making a game[6] about the Syrian refugee crisis that is seen in some quarters to trivialize a dire humanitarian crisis, although others consider it a perfectly logical evolution of the interactivity of modern journalism. "The idea that in the future, news will be played rather than read is quite hard for some people to think about," says Janet Jones, a professor of journalism at London South Bank University.[7] Yet that concept is really not at all hard for a generation reared on gaming, a generation that also needs to care about the news in some form, if journalism is to prosper and still do its job.)

Remarkably, for all the noise created by social, the life expectancy of serious journalism looks to be a lot longer than the life expectancy of legacy media suggests. Technology might actually be journalism's saviour. Jeff Jarvis said in a keynote address that journalism isn't dead. "What's dead is the business model for mass media." Jarvis, a professor at the City University of New York (CUNY) Graduate School of Journalism, is the author most recently of the book *Geeks Bearing Gifts: Imagining New Futures for News*.[8] His basic thesis is that legacy media are failing precisely because their business models depended on viewing their audience as a mostly ignorant mass, with editors and reporters dumbing down the world's complexity into easily digestible content they thought was all we deserved or could handle.

This no longer works when a lot of content is cheap to create, easy to find, and mostly free to access. The media that succeed in the future, Jarvis says, will act less like content providers and more like *service providers* who find out what communities need to function more successfully and then, where appropriate, apply the tools of journalism in service of those aims. The digital revolution will make it easier for journalism to respond to people's concerns, and journalism will be judged less by volume than by the value it creates. Jarvis states in his book: "Content is that which fills something. Service is that which accomplishes something. To be a service, news must be concerned with outcomes rather than products."[9] Interestingly, CUNY now offers a degree program in what it calls "social journalism." As aspirational as all this might sound, there is evidence that people are willing to pay for good journalism that addresses the issues they're interested in.

Consider the example of *De Correspondent*, in the Netherlands. A couple of years ago, two prominent Dutch journalists decided to quit their posts at traditional newspapers and launch a website where, in the words of publisher Ernst-Jan Pfauth, "We make journalism we believe in, and our members buy it." Simple as that. They crowd-funded an astonishing $1.7 million in a month (the first $1.3 million in just eight days), charging €60 for a one-year membership, but also inviting readers to donate as well as subscribe. Many did. *De Correspondent* doesn't take any advertising, and it doesn't have any institutional investors, meaning "We don't have to take any other stakeholders into account"—just readers, Pfauth said. *De Correspondent* steers clear of "news" reporting, since you can find burning buildings or flamed-out celebrities anywhere. Instead of focusing on what is unusual from one day to the next, "We try to write about things that happen *every* day." They write long-form, often investigative pieces about systemic issues, rather than symptomatic ones. And, most tellingly, they eschew the pulpit in favour of a platform that is purpose-built for the exchange of ideas. "Our journalists are conversation leaders," Pfauth said, "and our members are contributing experts." Journalists as curators, in other words, and comments as content, rather than being dark matter generated by cranks and trolls. By crowd-funding, *De Correspondent* consciously set out to "start a movement," not just a publication, and having grown membership and revenues since the initial flush of interest, the model seems to make the case that people will pay for journalistic symphonies, not just jingles.

More evidence comes in the form of Blendle, another Dutch startup that has been christened the "iTunes for news." Co-founder Alexander Klöpping was a technology reporter at a well-regarded newspaper when he came to realize that "none of what I was writing was getting read by my peers." Klöpping is in his twenties, and people in their twenties for the most part don't read newspapers (one study shows that when millennials hear about news, usually on social media, 57 per cent of those who want to know more go straight to a search engine; 5 per cent go to newspapers).[10] Not just in the Netherlands, but in Canada and elsewhere, blame for a growing democratic deficit is assigned to young people's lack of interest in public affairs, which is further equated to their lack of interest in newspapers. Young people don't much trust institutions, and they especially don't trust governments "now that politicians aren't exactly achieving anything," as Felix Salmon, senior editor of Fusion, told one session in Perugia. By extension, young people also don't trust, or just aren't interested in, politicians' bedfellows of yore, mainstream media.

Klöpping's team hit upon a deft way to repackage existing media into what he calls a "completely frictionless" platform that allows people to pay only for the news they consume. You may not want to read every story in the *New York Times,* or *De Telegraaf,* but that's what conventional sites ask you to do. You subscribe to a whole paper, labour away to choose what you want to read, and throw out the rest. But on Blendle you simply pay, per article, for what you read. It costs the equivalent of just 15 to 40 cents per article, and you can ask for a refund if you don't like the story (about 5 per cent of stories trigger requests for refunds)—the idea behind the enterprise being that, in Klöpping's words, "Just as there is Spotify for music and Netflix for movies, you now have Blendle for news." Young readers, he claims, are paying for news for the first time, and "Those are the people I want to get. Two-thirds of Blendle users are under 35."

What is fascinating, and heartening, is that "news doesn't sell well on Blendle, long-form does." Whether Blendle helps or hinders big media players in the long run, paywalls have mostly failed because they extend the idea that people want the whole hymn book. Allowing micropayments for specific content speaks to the appetites of individuals, not masses. Whether Blendle is sustainable, and whether it can work in the English-speaking world as opposed to the small and quite particular media market that is the Netherlands—those and other questions are up for debate. The site derives its ongoing revenues via licensing and revenue shares with the news organizations whose material it features (split 70:30 between the news organization and Blendle). The *New York Times* and German publishing giant Axel Springer were sufficiently impressed that they bet about $4 million between them on Blendle, which expanded into Germany in 2015 and soon boasted about 650,000 users in the Netherlands and Germany.[11] Blendle launched a beta version in the US in March 2016,[12] featuring content partners that include the *New York Times,* the *Wall Street Journal, Fast Company, Mother Jones, Barron's, FT Weekend, Newsweek,* the *Economist,* and one of the better experiments in web-based long-form journalism, the *Atavist Magazine.* It is charging 25 cents per story. Blendle, incidentally, partly owes its existence to a €200,000 grant for innovative journalism provided by the Democracy and Media Foundation,[13] which, like Canada's Inspirit Foundation, was itself funded through the proceeds of a media company sale.

If Klöpping and Co. have begun to crack the nut on what is now a perennial question in journalism—how to attract and keep millennials, who are the readers, watchers, and indeed players (not to mention voters) of the future—then maybe that's a ray of hope. Maybe all this crowd-funded, crowd-sourced disaggregation of content and disruption of legacy media is good news for journalism. Here in Canada, the *Winnipeg Free Press* has latched on to the micropayment idea, putting its website behind a paywall in 2015 (ho-hum) but offering up an alternative to its $16.99 monthly plan through a micropayment option that charges

27 cents per story. "What we've found is that there's a lot more engagement for the people who are on the site," said publisher Bob Cox.[14] "They're spending more time with stories." While digital sales thus far account for just 2 per cent of the *Free Press*'s revenue, that offsets losses in print circulation and offers a low-cost way to attract new readers, and revenues, to the paper. "We really see pay-per-article as our route to new readers," Cox said.

Back in Perugia, a session on new business models naturally featured *De Correspondent* and Blendle and referenced other digital start-ups in Europe, including two German sites, *Krautreporter* and *Correct!v*; Hungary's *Direkt36*; Iceland's *Stundin;* Sweden's *Blank Spot Project*, etc. The common theme that emerged was not just the extent to which new media organizations were turning to crowd-funding, but the emphasis on treating readers as *members.* That requires a level of service and attention that is unprecedented and expensive, but one that the founders of these sites believe is absolutely essential for gaining loyalty and retaining it. "Journalism should be a conversation," said the *Guardian*'s Pilhofer, echoing Pfauth.

On *Guardian* for thee

FROM PERUGIA, I went to London and to the *Guardian* itself, a bastion of liberal/progressive journalism that, while watching its daily print sales decline to just under 175,000 papers in 2015,[15] saw online growth expand to nearly 9 million daily readers in early 2016.[16] It rivals the

New York Times, Le Monde, and *Der Spiegel* for influence, and arguably exceeds them all. The *Guardian* is a child of the Scott Trust, which has assets of approximately £700 million and whose core purpose is

> To secure the financial and editorial independence of the Guardian in perpetuity: as a quality national newspaper without party affiliation; remaining faithful to its liberal tradition; as a profit-seeking enterprise managed in an efficient and cost-effective manner.[17]

The closest any legacy media organization in Canada comes to articulating a social purpose so explicitly, other than the CBC, is the *Toronto Star*, which is guided by the Atkinson Principles:[18]

- A strong, united and independent Canada
- Social justice
- Individual and civil liberties
- Community and civic engagement
- The rights of working people
- The necessary role of government

But for all its good intentions, the *Toronto Star* pales in comparison to the *Guardian* when it comes to delivering on its principles.

What is interesting about the *Guardian* is not just that it has such a large online following worldwide, but that under former editor Alan Rusbridger, it became a clarion of advocacy and campaign journalism that is arguably without equal anywhere in the English-speaking world. Among its recent and most celebrated achievements are its reporting on Edward Snowden's revelations about government eavesdropping, and starting in early 2015, a huge and relentless campaign focused on climate change called Keep It in the Ground. The paper campaigned hard (in partnership with an NGO, 350.org) to force fossil-fuel producers to cut their activities back to a level that gives the world a chance to stay below the two degrees of warming that is thought to be the level below which we might still successfully adapt to climate change. To do that, about 80 per cent of known fossil-fuel reserves need to be written off as "stranded assets," and massive investments must be made in renewables. To accelerate that transition, the *Guardian* has championed divestment from fossil fuels. The newspaper targeted the Gates Foundation and Britain's Wellcome Trust, and thus far has more than 200,000 reader signatures asking these globally significant charities to divest. This is a no-holds-barred bit of pamphleteering in the greatest tradition of crusading journalism, and it says something about the paleness of Canadian journalism that among our supposedly mainstream media, nobody comes anywhere near as close to calling our energy sector (and our investment community) to account.

In Perugia, Dan Gillmor, who teaches digital media literacy at Arizona State University's Walter Cronkite School of Journalism and Mass Communication, spoke strongly in support of advocacy media.

In many parts of the world, doing real journalism is activism—because truth-telling in some societies is an act designed to bring about change... exposing injustices with the absolute goal of stirring public anger, and then public action to bring about change... Even those journalists who worship at the altar of objectivity should recognize that on at least some issues, they cannot possibly be objective. Or at least, they should not be. On some issues we have to take stands, even though those stands may put us at policy odds with the people and institutions we cover.

For his part, Rusbridger—who calls climate change "the biggest story in the world"—is unapologetic about mixing reporting and advocacy in pursuit of that story. He says science so clearly favours those who claim that our civilization is threatened over the arguments of climate-change deniers that "pretending that these are equally balanced arguments is actually a form of distortion itself." Rusbridger did an interview with CBC Radio on May 10, 2015, and it's worth spending half an hour to hear him out.[19] Otherwise, the Coles Notes are that he makes a lucid and erudite argument not just for divestment and for the need to treat climate change much more seriously, but for the importance of journalism in public life. He admits no one has yet found a silver bullet for funding new media, and he agrees that threats to traditional media are indeed dire, but he also says there are still some "brilliant things going on." He feels that new ways of reaching audiences, data mining, combining media, connecting with audiences by giving them ways to provide feedback, crowd-sourcing, and citizen journalism make this "really the most exciting time in journalism... the overriding change, the overriding need for journalism... the centrality of journalism is more important than ever. When a town loses its newspaper, it's like losing its police force or its ambulance service or its fire service. At its best, journalism is a completely necessary, important part of the mix of what a society is."

It's that sensibility, and the *Guardian*'s interest in expanding its values-based journalism model internationally, that led me to London with a question: could or would the *Guardian* expand into Canada? I didn't meet with Rusbridger, but I did talk to two senior members of his staff: Tony Danker (chief strategy officer) and Ben Hicks (then head of grants and research). Note that the *Guardian* has, in addition to its UK and international editions, created bespoke editions in the United States and Australia, and has talked of plans to increase reporting resources in India. I was pleasantly surprised to hear they have thought about Canada. "I've been looking at Canada for three years," Danker said.

The Australian edition, he said, came about for two reasons: the dominance of Rupert Murdoch and Fairfax Media, which drives out competition and renders the media landscape there monocultural; and the fact that they had a philanthropist/investor (Graeme Wood) to grease the skids with an amount of money Danker wouldn't reveal, but which Wood himself later told me was in excess of $20 million AUS—not a grant, but an investment. Wood had previously funded, and then turned sour on, a sort of gold-standard journalism product in Australia called the *Global Mail*. After that failed to really take off, he pulled his money and plowed what was left, and then some, into helping the *Guardian* land in Oz.[20]

As to Canada, Danker's initial observation was that the media concentration/quality issues are not as dire here as in Australia (I disabused him of that notion), and there is a complication in that some Canadians read the US edition. That said, he recognizes that Canadians would likely rally to a Canadian edition of the *Guardian*. He and Hicks made it clear that deciding to come to Canada would be easier if something like the Australian scenario played out. In Danker's words, "I would love to find a Canadian Graeme Wood."

On a personal visit to Australia in October 2015, I met with Wood at his Sydney office. He declared himself to be pleased with the social impact of *Guardian Australia*, which he felt had "changed the tone" of discourse in the country. However, "financially it hasn't met expectations." Display advertising "fell into a hole globally" just as *Guardian Australia* launched, with YouTube, Google, and Facebook ripping up the market playbook right before Wood's eyes. Wood thinks a *Guardian Canada* would be a good idea. As for a "Canadian Graeme Wood," the

Australian one says: "If they do it because it's a good thing to do, that's pretty cool. If they do it to make a buck, they might be waiting awhile."

In fact, one criticism of the *Guardian*—not just in Australia, but globally—is that while its quality is indisputable, its profligacy is unsustainable. Or as John Stackhouse wrote in *Mass Disruption* after visiting the *Guardian*'s offices near King's Cross, it's a nice place to be "if you don't have a mortgage to pay. Much like the organization." For all that it is backed by the Scott Trust, Stackhouse said, it was also "losing so much money that some staff feared the trust would soon run out."[21] That seems unlikely, but it would certainly seem to constrain any meteoric growth in its international ambitions. And it is not as if simply getting a *Guardian Canada* off the ground would magically solve the problems of Canadian journalism. Still, more *Guardian* in Canada—in whatever form—would help improve quality and turn up the volume on progressive thought and action here. As Penelope Jones, then head of international business development for Guardian News & Media, observed in an internal paper on Canada's media landscape,

Canada's legacy newspapers, fighting for survival, are heavily dependent on big business and an aging, conservative readership. The response to the digital age has been defensive. Canada's young progressives are actively seeking a media outlet more in tune with the open web.

Canada needs a national, progressive, open, digital platform. Canada needs a new plurality to help translate the
outcomes of a key election. Canada needs media not in
thrall to the energy or corporate sectors.[22]

The *Guardian* isn't coming to Canada anytime soon
without a source of funds to support its entry into our market, although it did not go unnoticed, Jones says, that "our
[the *Guardian*'s Canadian] election coverage received an
incredibly high volume of traffic from Canada." A *Guardian* correspondent in Spain, Ashifa Kassam, meanwhile,
moved home to Toronto in 2016 to start work as the *Guardian*'s first dedicated Canada correspondent.[23]

THREE

What's Happening Closer to Home?

IN THE SPIRIT of one of my favourite short stories, Raymond Carver's "So Much Water So Close to Home," I figured I should fish around in North America for a bit, to test the waters of media innovation closer to home. In particular, it seemed worthwhile to examine what is or isn't happening in the world of philanthropy, given well-established American foundation support for journalism and media innovation there. What might Canadian foundations learn from their much larger and better-capitalized peers to the south? And what, if anything, was already happening in that sector here?

In March 2015, the Walter and Duncan Gordon Foundation sponsored a symposium, Confronting Complexity,[1] at Massey College, where few bright rays pierced the gloom of a snoozefest introduced by Stephen Toope and featuring

John Cruickshank (*Toronto Star*), David Walmsley (*Globe and Mail*), and Anna Maria Tremonti (CBC Radio).[2] Given that a federal election was just months away, much of the discussion focused on political reporting and audience engagement. Toope, director of the Munk School of Global Affairs at the University of Toronto, mainly concerned himself with what he saw as a growing disconnect between Canadian citizens and their political institutions. With fewer media-led public convenings and less media influence (note that his comments came *before* the federal Conservatives said they wouldn't participate in traditional election debates hosted by CBC/CTV/Global), Toope expressed fears that mobilizing the electorate was "critical" but that "private actions" in the digital realm were unlikely to be enough to sustain community engagement. Cruickshank claimed that media are "responsible for the great bulk of civic knowledge in society," yet he also said, discouragingly, "I don't see communicating complex policy issues as a particular strength of the media." Given that the demographic profile of news consumers and voters is virtually identical, he said, in the current media climate the "loss of Canadian self-knowledge and a lack of participation ... [is] going to get a lot, lot worse."

Walmsley made a point that will be echoed below, which is that journalism "isn't in decline," although he didn't really offer any evidence other than to say that there are more people using news all the time. Tremonti made another point that will resound below: "I tell young journalists

they have to come up with a new business model." At the
symposium, perhaps the best comments came not from
the journalists but from Hilary Pearson, president of Philanthropic Foundations Canada, who in a separate panel
discussion averred that Canadian foundations are too ner-
vous to get into public debates and seem to shy away from
taking a stand. "We alleviate, but we don't *prevent* poverty.
We educate, but we don't *advocate.*" Young people, she said,
want to *solve* problems, not just talk about them (or write
about them). In the end, the symposium was only dimly
illuminating, and wholly discouraging. Some of the top
names in the leading media voices of the land offered little more than assurances that the demand for news isn't
about to go away, with precious little insight into where
new business models are going to come from. Apparently,
some combination of youth and technology will come to
our rescue.

IN SUBSEQUENT MONTHS, I spent some time in Toronto,
Boston, New York, and of course Vancouver, where I am
based. In Canada, the news from Postmedia was getting
worse and reports from virtually every other corner of the
Canadian media landscape were bleak. South of the border, by contrast, the *New York Times*, which spends $300
million USD a year on journalism, in August reached the
milestone of having more than one million digital-only
subscribers.[3] Mark Thompson, president and CEO of the
New York Times Company, predicted that within five years,

digital revenue could surpass print revenue. "I think five years is feasible to reach that tipping point," Thompson said. On the same day that Thompson marked the *Times'* digital milestone, the CEO of Axel Springer, Europe's largest newspaper publisher, was reported as saying the future for his company will be English-speaking and *entirely digital*. Mathias Döpfner, a former music critic, said in an interview that within a decade, newspapers will only exist "as a kind of... vintage item," much like vinyl records.[4] "Digital journalism should be and could be and will be much better than printed journalism."

In search of further insights and promising developments closer to home than Berlin, I talked to a number of observers and practitioners in North America, not just about journalism but about philanthropy's role in advancing media innovation in Canada. What follows is drawn in part from interviews I conducted with them in 2015.

Erin Millar, Discourse Media (Vancouver)

Discourse Media is a rare bright light in the collaborative, solutions-based media landscape. (Disclosure: in early 2016, I began providing the company with strategic advice.) It currently functions as a production company, producing and enabling major journalism projects on complex issues. Its content is distributed on its own digital platforms and also through social media and in partnership with existing media outlets ranging from legacy players like the *Globe and Mail* to Al Jazeera to regional publications such as the *Dhaka Tribune* and *Metro Halifax*.

A good example of how Discourse adds value to existing media outlets is a February 18, 2016, feature in *Maclean's* magazine, "Canada's prisons are the 'new residential schools.'"[5] The report was written by *Maclean's* associate editor Nancy Macdonald and is a searing account of how poorly Canada's justice system treats indigenous people. Some of the on-the-ground reporting, along with a survey of more than 850 post-secondary students in Regina, Saskatoon, and Winnipeg, and the subsequent data analysis, was done by Discourse in close partnership with Macdonald and her editors. Embedded in the story is a piece by Discourse Media co-founder Erin Millar[6] explaining that the survey results "provide quantitative evidence, where very little data exists, that isolated reports of racial profiling may be a common systemic issue." For geeks, there is a five-page technical brief that explains the survey methodology.[7]

This is emblematic of what good journalism is beginning to look like in the digital age: projects produced by a team of journalists, data analysts, designers, and engagement specialists that are commissioned by media outlets (which increasingly lack the capacity to produce major projects as they lay off more of their core staff) or are funded by foundations, non-profits, corporate sponsors, or individuals through crowd-funding campaigns. Discourse Media enables in-depth journalism at other outlets by partnering with journalists through fellowships, training, consulting, and initiating other sorts of partnerships that reallocate resources.

While not exclusively investigative in its approach, Discourse is focused on innovation in journalism practice. As Millar says, "We don't want to produce a really good version of the traditional form, but actually a new approach leveraging innovative digital storytelling forms; use reporting methods that allow us to be much more relevant to our communities; use data in a much smarter way; collaborate with researchers and others to improve how we report on science; and ensure all our work is driven by intentional impact and is mindful of how it influences public discourse."

Discourse puts a great deal of effort into engagement activities aimed at extending the impact of journalism content from the pages of its media partners into communities that are grappling with the issues it reports on. It leverages partnerships in a way that comes closest in Canada to what ProPublica (see below) does in the US, with a little Solutions Journalism Network thrown in (also see below).

Discourse Media has thus far attracted modest foundation resources, gearing more to project-based work with publications and NGOs on issues including global energy poverty; networking underrepresented communities in Western Canada through web and mobile platforms; harnessing student journalists to report on diverse visions of Canada's future; integrating solutions journalism frameworks into new media models; and access to healthy food. A multi-year project on Reconciliation aims to make a significant contribution to Canada's ability to rethink its national narrative around indigenous people.

While these are early days, Discourse Media—still shy of its third birthday—has ambitious growth plans that involve transitioning from a production house to becoming a larger player in the Canadian media landscape. It is as close as anything I have seen or heard about that aligns with CUNY professor Jeff Jarvis's vision of treating journalism less like some kind of highbrow profession where journalists are ordained and more like a service for which they are trained to respond to community needs. As Discourse's website states: "We collaborate with a wide range of organizations and communities that are rich sources of data and narratives... We function as a one-stop freelance shop where media outlets can commission editorial, data analysis and interactives, infographics and digital content. We also provide workshops, training and consulting on data journalism, community-based reporting and engagement."[8] Sounds a lot like a service to me.

Duncan McCue, UBC Graduate School of Journalism (Vancouver)

A national correspondent with CBC TV in Vancouver, Duncan McCue is Anishinaabe, a member of the Chippewas of Georgina Island First Nation in southern Ontario. He is an adjunct professor in UBC's Graduate School of Journalism, where he teaches a course on reporting in indigenous communities. In 2011, he was awarded a Knight fellowship at Stanford University, where he developed an online guide to reporting in indigenous communities.[9] In McCue's view, one obviously coloured by his experience as the beneficiary of a US reporting fellowship, there is a "shameful lack" of philanthropic support for journalism in Canada. He has a long list of things he believes could support better journalism in, by, and about indigenous communities: online journalism training, cultural competency training, travel grants, boot camps for indigenous reporters, and other supports to change the conversation about indigenous issues, especially in light of Call to Action #86 of the Truth and Reconciliation Commission: "We call upon Canadian journalism programs and media schools to require education for all students on the history of Aboriginal peoples, including the history and legacy of residential schools, the *United Nations Declaration on the Rights of Indigenous Peoples*, Treaties and Aboriginal rights, Indigenous law, and Aboriginal-Crown relations."[10]

Andrea Nemtin, Inspirit Foundation (Toronto)

Nemtin is president and CEO of the Inspirit Foundation, which was born in 2012 out of the proceeds of the sale of Vision TV two years earlier.[11] "We need to ensure that media remains democratic," Nemtin told me. "To make change, we need a greater representation of voices across all media platforms." Naturally, given its lineage, the Inspirit Foundation has focused on the role that media and arts, including journalism, play in creating positive social change.

With an increasing number of story-based knowledge-sharing platforms, "The process and possibilities for engaging in shaping more nuanced, inclusive, and democratic social narratives have dramatically increased," Nemtin said. "Young change leaders are at the forefront of utilizing these platforms in really interesting and impactful ways."

Thus far, Inspirit has supported a number of story-based projects across the country of various scales, topics, and intended audiences. One example is Cinema Politica, a Montreal-based non-profit network of community and campus organizations that screens independent political film and video. "We were so proud to fund a group of screenings and conversations which enabled both activists and media makers to explore the connection between spirituality and social justice," Nemtin said.

The foundation is also deeply committed to supporting young change leaders who are just starting out and working in local contexts. Hence its support for Tusma Sulieman, an emerging media maker passionate about addressing Islamophobia. Sulieman proposed working with Regent Park Focus, a non-profit participatory media organization that supports young people considered "at risk" or "marginalized" in telling bold, new stories. "It makes perfect sense to support more democratic journalism projects, which will enable young change leaders to shape narratives that will ultimately shape the society that they will inherit," Nemtin said. "When it comes to issues of inclusion, it's important to create space within the industry for people to tell their own stories... to not simply be written about but to

reclaim their histories, to celebrate their everyday achievements, and to express their aspirations in their own words
on their own terms. We're especially interested in the ways
journalism can support Reconciliation and also address
Islamophobia—two of our priority issue areas."

Meanwhile, Nemtin pointed me to Media Impact
Funders in the US,[12] whose website says: "Increasingly,
foundations are supporting journalism projects—to bol-
ster local and statehouse coverage, illuminate pressing
social issues, or ensure that governments and corporations remain accountable. However, when it comes time to
evaluate the outcomes of those investments, conflicts with
fiercely independent newsrooms can arise."[13] That organization has produced a tool for measuring funder impact on
media.

Nemtin was en route to a conference in San Francisco,
the Media Impact Forum. Among the many things to note
from a recap of the forum[14] was the work of Van Jones
(working with the late singer Prince) to found #YesWeCode,
an initiative aimed at training 100,000 low-opportunity
youth to become high-level coders. Could something
analogous work in Canada with Aboriginal kids? Also
at the forum, craigslist founder Craig Newmark shared
an insightful quote from one of his high school teachers,
who said, "A trustworthy press is the immune system of
democracy." Inspirit is working to ensure that Canada's
democratic immune system includes Islamic and indigenous voices.

Robert Steiner, Munk School of
Global Affairs (Toronto)

Steiner is a former foreign correspondent for the *Wall Street Journal* and recipient of two Overseas Press Club Awards; he was part of a small *WSJ* reporting team that were finalists for a Pulitzer Prize in International Reporting in 1996. Steiner now works in Toronto as director of fellowships in global journalism at the Munk School of Global Affairs. What he has put together at Munk is one of the most interesting things going on in journalism education in the country. Rather than train entry-level journalists to enter a field that is shrinking in size, opportunity, and impact, Munk takes early- and mid-career subject-matter specialists—and even a few at later stages of their careers—and trains them to use journalism to advance public policy reform through the media. Steiner runs an eight-month program that begins with a five-week boot camp in Toronto, during which fellows learn the fundamentals of responsible journalism. After the boot camp, fellows return to their bases around the world and cover their specialties—with mentorship from senior journalists and program advisers—for major news organizations with which Munk is partnered, including the *Globe and Mail*, *CBC News*, Postmedia, the *Dallas Morning News*, the *Boston Globe*, the *Deseret News National Edition*, and *Foreign Policy*.

For a program that's only been around since 2012, the results are impressive.[15] In the first three years, Munk's 39 fellows had more than 400 pieces published and aired in major media before graduating from their fellowship. One of their alumni, Dr. Seema Yasmin, was nominated for the Pulitzer Prize within a year of graduating for her work covering health at the *Dallas Morning News*. Another fellow, Anna Nicolaou, was awarded the Overseas Press Club Foundation's 2014 prize as one of 14 of America's most promising foreign correspondents (she is now working at the *Financial Times*). A third, Alia Dharssi, received Postmedia's Michelle Lang Fellowship, the most prestigious award for a starting journalist in Canada. And a fourth, Michael Kempa, received an honourable mention for investigative reporting from Canada's National Magazine Awards for a *Walrus* piece he did investigating governance problems in the RCMP.

Peter Klein, International Reporting Program (Vancouver)

On the West Coast, University of British Columbia Graduate School of Journalism associate professor Peter Klein, a former *60 Minutes* producer, snagged a $1 million grant for his International Reporting Program from Alison Lawton and her Mindset Social Innovation Foundation.[16] Klein deploys journalism students overseas to produce "major works of global journalism" investigating the international electronic waste trade (which earned his team an Emmy for Best Investigative Newsmagazine) and other issues such as access to medical morphine, shrimp farming in

Thailand, violent land disputes in Brazil, and the emerging environmental movement in China.[17] Ultimately, according to Klein, "The goal of the IRP is to grow into a larger, more ambitious Global Reporting Centre, which would continue teaching international reporting, but would also bring together some of the top global journalists to tackle major projects on [under-covered] global issues."[18] The Centre, which launched in June 2016, would benefit from philanthropic backing.

April Lindgren, Ryerson University School of Journalism (Toronto)

Most professional journalists I have been speaking to believe, admittedly with the benefit of hindsight, that most J-schools are production lines for pretty low-grade journalism education. Whether or not that's true, these schools also produce research, and the most interesting work I'm aware of at Ryerson is being conducted by associate professor April Lindgren, who has been studying the presence and effects of what she calls "local news poverty" in population centres that have lost their main media voices. In a seminar, she noted that a CRTC survey in 2013 found that

> 81 per cent of respondents identified local news as more important than any other type of content including national or international news, feature films or sports. While Canada's major cities are served by myriad local news sources, the story in smaller cities, suburban areas,

and rural municipalities is more problematic. In many of these communities, local news choices are becoming more limited as local outlets disappear, consolidate or shut down. In Thunder Bay, Ontario, CBC Radio's local drive-home show was recently cancelled and replaced by a program broadcast out of Sudbury. Red Deer, Alberta, with a population of nearly 100,000, remains one of the largest Canadian cities outside a major metropolitan market to operate without a TV station following the 2009 closure of the local CanWest station.[19]

Lindgren's Local News Research Project[20] includes creating a map of media closures, consolidations, and openings across Canada that will help track national patterns; and, in the communities of Brampton, Oakville, City of Kawartha Lakes, Peterborough, and Thunder Bay (Ontario), Brandon (Manitoba), as well as Nanaimo and Kamloops (BC), she conducted "web scraping" in order to assess the availability of news about local electoral races for Members of Parliament; to discover reasons for any differences in news availability; to analyze the effects of social media; and to survey whether people had enough information to vote in an informed way. Lindgren's research is ongoing and worth watching.

Joshua Benton, Nieman Lab
(Cambridge, Massachusetts)

Benton is a dedicated Canada-phile who heads up the Nieman Lab at Harvard, "a project [of the Nieman Foundation] to try to help figure out where the news is headed in the Internet age." The Nieman Foundation's mission is "to promote and elevate the standards of journalism," which it does through Nieman Reports (covering thought leadership), Nieman Lab, and Nieman Storyboard (the art and craft of reported storytelling). In Canada, journalists look with envy at the resources that the Nieman Foundation devotes to journalistic excellence. Some Canadian journalists benefit from this by becoming Nieman fellows: a Canadian is selected for the program once every second year, the most recent being Laura-Julie Perreault from *La Presse*. The Canadian fellowship is sponsored by the Martin Wise Goodman Trust out of Toronto.

Nieman Lab, meanwhile, operates as a newsroom that focuses on news innovation. Benton says 90 per cent of its content is US-focused. In 2015, it devoted two stories to examining, first, *La Presse*'s bet on shifting from print to tablet, and, one week later, the *Toronto Star*'s decision to pursue its own digital Holy Grail through *Star Touch*. The Nieman Lab report[21] said the *Star* was wagering there is a "big pot of potential new revenue [in] higher-priced digital advertising," although Benton told me he is "more pessimistic about digital ads than I've ever been." Or as Tom Standage, deputy editor of the *Economist* has said, "The *Economist* has taken the view that advertising is nice, and we'll certainly take money where we can get it, but we're pretty much expecting it to go away."[22] Anyway, this is just a sliver of the sorts of insights that are the bread and butter of Nieman Lab, which has no real equivalent in Canada.

The Nieman Foundation devotes all its assets (approximately $140 million USD) to improving journalism, and there certainly is no equivalent to that in Canada.

Benton is keen to do more than just keep a weather eye on Canadian journalism. "We could bring together some of our own experts and others to assemble a curriculum around what would be most useful for Canada's current/ future journalism leaders to know. That could include discussions with American industry leaders on strategy; training on specific topics like building an innovative organization, design thinking, and entrepreneurship; and perhaps some sort of project that attendees would bring back to their work to execute on. I could imagine a group of 10 to 20 people, perhaps selected from an open call for applications that reaches a wide range of Canadian media workers... You'd also be building a new community of future journalism leaders by having them share this sort of an experience." I would add a fourth option, which is that Nieman could curate and host, on behalf of Canadian foundations or interested investors, a media change lab that could dig deep into the strengths and weaknesses of the many options and approaches identified in this book.

StoryCorps (New York)

I was drawn to StoryCorps after hearing of the US-based oral history project[23] when its founder, Dave Isay, won the $1 million TED Prize at the 2015 TED conference in Vancouver. StoryCorps' central idea is to record conversations, often between family members—sometimes extraordinary conversations, often not—and have them archived at the Library of Congress, with a small number edited down and broadcast on NPR in the US. The recordings originally took place in booths, with 40 minutes usually condensed to about 4; there's now an app that allows people to record a conversation for StoryCorps anywhere. A number of non-profit and community organizations now contract Story-Corps to record conversations as a community-building function. As Isay told the *Globe and Mail*, it's "about communication and creating a world that listens a little better. And really I think that the core idea of StoryCorps is that every life matters equally... What's interesting to me is that you can have this conversation with someone who matters to you, and that 100 years from now, 200 years from now and 500 years from now, your great-great-great grandkids will get to understand a little bit about where they come from."[24]

Given that StoryCorps' mission is "to preserve and share humanity's stories in order to build connections between people and create a more just and compassionate world," I thought its way of using and archiving interviews between people was something that might contribute to the post–Truth and Reconciliation Commission work in Canada. Through its partnership with NPR (think CBC), StoryCorps reaches a wide audience. I met with Braden Lay-Michaels, chief external relations officer, and Lidy Chu, director of institutional giving, at the company's

Brooklyn headquarters. They told me that program evaluations revealed that StoryCorps interviews had been found to build empathy and understanding with listeners, and that the almost 500 community organizations with which the organization has partnered across the US themselves report positive impacts from the StoryCorps approach. Its "relentless focus on serving a wide diversity of participants" strikes me as something that is ideally suited to Canada.

Brielle Morgan, Storywise (Vancouver)

Given the potential I see in StoryCorps, I was all the more delighted to stumble upon its analogue in my hometown, where Brielle Morgan is piloting something she calls Storywise. Her goal is to "lead a collaborative search for impactful stories"[25] that might form the basis for podcasts, inspire art, spur deeper reporting about issues the interviews reveal, and more generally "create opportunities for people often marginalized to connect with each other and the community through stories." Morgan and her team reported positive feedback after doing their first formal story facilitations at the 39th annual BC Elders Gathering in Saanich, BC, in 2015, where 3,000-plus First Nations people gathered (Storywise was invited back in 2016). The Storywise approach seems like a natural fit not just for Aboriginal communities but also for immigrant communities, particularly in increasingly "atomized" cities like Vancouver, whose "well documented isolation problem," as

Morgan describes it, creates multiple challenges. Morgan has, in the interim at least, found a home at Discourse Media to expand upon her ideas.

David Bornstein, Solutions Journalism Network (New York)

Bornstein is a Canadian who heads up the Solutions Journalism Network in New York. It's hard not to like someone who starts a breakfast meeting with a quote from Chekhov: "Man will become better when you show him what he is like." From the website, Solutions "is increasing the volume and quality of solutions journalism through our online learning platform, journalism development, and community-building." Bornstein believes young people in particular are less interested in just reading/reporting bad news, and instead "want something that taps into their sense of agency. 'What can I do to solve this [issue] working with other people?'" Solutions is demand-driven, providing tool kits and workshops in newsrooms to help propagate the idea of solutions journalism, which, at its best,[26] combines good journalism practice with solution finding. In other words, you can write ad infinitum about discipline problems in Seattle schools, as the *Seattle Times* had, or more typically, just do one blockbuster story on a problem, supplemented by a couple of quick follow-ups, and then move on. Or, as the *Seattle Times* did in partnership with Solutions, you can set up an education lab to "test whether journalists can create solutions-oriented discourse by exploring remedies for the most urgent challenges facing public education,"[27] which, it turns out, you can. Again, journalism as a *service*.

Richard Tofel, ProPublica (New York)

One of the big success stories in digital journalism in the US is ProPublica. Its president since 2013 and general manager at its founding in 2007, Richard Tofel was previously a senior executive at the *Wall Street Journal* and Dow Jones & Co., and has published several books. ProPublica—"Journalism in the Public Interest"—is held up by many reporters as the gold standard for modern journalism; as it says, it's "an independent, non-profit newsroom that produces investigative journalism in the public interest. Our work focuses exclusively on truly important stories, stories with 'moral force.' We do this by producing journalism that shines a light on exploitation of the weak by the strong and on the failures of those with power to vindicate the trust placed in them"—in other words, comforting the afflicted and afflicting the comfortable.

They also do it with a lot of money: their annual budget is currently $12.5 million USD. The Sandler Foundation initially contributed about 90 per cent of ProPublica's funding; it now has more than 2,600 donors, and the Sandlers contribute about 25 per cent of the budget. ProPublica doesn't charge people to read its content because, as Tofel told me, "Restricting access to content doesn't support our mission." ProPublica, headquartered in Manhattan, has a newsroom of about 45 journalists, all dedicated to investigative reporting, which it contends is now seen by most media as an unaffordable luxury. At ProPublica, more than 75 cents out of every dollar is spent on news—"in stark contrast with traditional print news organizations, even very good ones, that devote about 15 cents of each dollar spent to news."[28]

Much of ProPublica's content is offered to traditional news organizations, free of charge, for publication or broadcast. Sometimes it is offered to heavy hitters like the *New York Times* or the *Washington Post*, but in other cases partners are selected for potential impact in a sector or a geographical area. ProPublica has had more than 120 publishing partners since its inception. Almost all of its stories are available for reprint under a Creative Commons licence. ProPublica made history in the US by winning the 2011 Pulitzer Prize for National Reporting, the first such prize ever given for stories not published in print. One of its stories was awarded a Pulitzer Prize for Investigative Reporting in 2010, the first such award won by an online news organization. Its site also features investigative reporting produced by others, making it both a destination and a tool for promoting good work in this field. Each story that ProPublica produces is backed up with "an active and aggressive communications effort of our own, including regularly contacting reporters, editors and bloggers, encouraging them to follow-up on our reporting, and to link to our site and our work."

In terms of impact, ProPublica maintains that "from a philanthropic perspective... our model assures an unusually high level of accountability for a non-profit. Our major stories have to be sufficiently compelling to convince editors and producers to accord them space or time. As they do so consistently, donors [can] be confident that professional standards are being met and maintained, and that important work is being undertaken. That said, our donors support the independence of our work, and do not influence our editorial processes." ProPublica accepts advertising and is exploring possible new revenue streams, including the sale of data and e-books, although philanthropy, large gifts and small, will continue to be its principal source of income for the foreseeable future. That said, Tofel told me, "We'd love to have an endowment."

ProPublica Canada? Tofel is cautious about exposing his own organization to "mission creep," so the case would have to be a compelling one. What would make it really compelling, similar to the *Guardian,* would be money. ProPublica has contemplated diversifying its efforts (in the US) to state/regional branch plants, so to speak, but it is unlikely to adopt that model without an "anchor funder" in each place. It would need that to contemplate extending its model into Canada, too.

John Bracken, Knight Foundation (Chicago)

The last group I'll profile is a very big fish. The Knight Foundation *spends* $120 million USD each year on journalism, media innovation, engaged communities, and the arts. Its website states, "We believe that democracy thrives when people and communities are informed and engaged."[29] Or as John Knight himself said in 1969, "Thus we seek to bestir the people into an awareness of their own condition, provide inspiration for their thoughts and rouse them to pursue their true interests."

Bracken is vice-president of media innovation at the foundation and oversees the Knight News Challenge and the Knight Prototype Fund. He says it's pretty hard to make bets on technology innovation because it is such a rapidly changing field: "You can't know what's going to happen in the next 12 to 24 months." Knight has placed its recent emphasis on being "a catalytic funder," and Bracken's preference is to back emerging leaders, "young, start-up focused leaders" like the folks behind Matter,[30] in San Francisco, who pose a disarmingly ambitious question: "What if we tried to build the next great, meaningful media institutions from scratch?"

Matter offers $50,000 USD to help build "scalable media ventures with a human-centered, prototype-driven design process" in which promising ideas are road-tested over five months. It is, of course, just one among many bright lights in the Knight sky. Knight has invested in Pro-Publica, it funds Nieman Lab, it is funding the *Guardian* in the US to the tune of $2.6 million USD to establish an innovation lab to develop new approaches to delivering news and information on mobile technology. Knight funded 8 80 Cities, which is where, inevitably, one again encounters Discourse Media, whose Doable City Reader[31] focuses on urban transformation. Knight funded a second phase of collaboration between 8 80 Cities and Discourse Media, expanding the reader, applying community-based reporting methods to 8 80 Cities' engagement strategy, and bringing in Discourse Media's solutions journalists to mentor Knight fellows who are interested in integrating storytelling into their urban intervention work. Lots of Canadians, meanwhile, have been selected as Knight fellows.

Bracken, like Joshua Benton at Nieman Lab, believes that finding ways to support local journalism remains the biggest challenge in all jurisdictions. Full participation in democracy, Bracken says, requires that citizens have access to news and information, yet "we have consistently seen growing disinterest in elections, especially at the local level." The Knight News Challenge has, over the past eight years, invested $50 million USD in more than 130 projects that experiment with new ways of producing and sharing information. In 2015, the News Challenge distributed $3.2 million USD to 22 winning applications focused on elections and elections coverage.[32] Some of these will be supported through the separate but related vehicle of the Knight Prototype Fund—what Bracken refers to as a kind of innovation "inbox" at the foundation—which provides $35,000 to media innovators, who are given six months "to research, test core assumptions and iterate before building out an entire project,"[33] which may or may not attract further Knight funding and/or investment.

The kind of ecosystem that Knight provides for journalism is something we can only dream about in Canada, although Bracken said he is open to exploring how the infrastructure and methodologies (not to mention the experience) that Knight brings to the table could be deployed through a partnership with one or more motivated Canadian foundations. Now there's a thought.

Be Online or on Life-Support

BACK IN CANADA, when people look for an antidote to the death throes of our outdated media business models,[34] they of course turn to the Internet—both blaming it for so massively undercutting traditional media models and lionizing its potential to be the media's saviour. With the extirpation of newspapers well underway, and with the *Star*'s flawed fascination with tablets worthy of an 11th Commandment—"Don't!"—the future of independent, public-interest journalism in Canada is assuredly off-tablet but otherwise online, and mostly on people's phones.

So far in Canada, examples of independent news websites that might stand the test of the media's radically disrupted times are few and far between. *Huffington Post Canada* would seem to be the most robust success story, but only because of considerable backing by US giant AOL,[35] which purchased HuffPo for $315 million. The

Canadian arm would not survive if the US arm folded. And yet, for all its resources, *Huffington Post Canada* produces very little original Canadian content. And although it provides a few new media jobs in Canada, they are far too few to offset other losses. In 2015, BuzzFeed opened a bureau in Toronto,[36] which, again, meant a few more media jobs, but they can hardly be confused with journalism.

Homegrown examples of independent experiments include the Vancouver-based *Tyee*[37] (to which I contribute an occasional column) and Toronto-based Rabble,[38] avowedly progressive websites that owe their survival to funding tied to the labour movement. Both started over a decade ago and receive between 500,000 and a million page views a month, a fraction of what the *Globe and Mail* or even the *Vancouver Sun* receive. Another long-running experiment is the *Vancouver Observer*,[39] which has ties to US foundation money and the environmental movement. In 2014, Ricochet was launched after a crowd-funding campaign on Indiegogo raised $83,000. In the fall of 2015, a further $16,000 was crowd-funded for Ricochet's Indigenous Reporting Fund. According to one of Ricochet's editors, Ethan Cox, the bulk of Ricochet's working revenue comes from recurring monthly donations, or memberships, of $5, $10, or $25; it gets additional revenue from advertising and sponsorships, and ongoing support from the Caisse Populaire Desjardins in Quebec and other sponsors.

Ricochet bills itself as an "audacious response"[40] to the meltdown in Canadian media, promising (and delivering) investigative journalism and activist commentary, on both French and English platforms, for a "plurinational Canada." According to Cox, "Ricochet never had an angel backer, and everything we've built has been done through individual contributions averaging between 5 and 10 dollars." With its editors mostly working unpaid, Ricochet is able to pay a minimum of $100 for each journalistic piece it publishes— in keeping, Cox said, with a model that, "from the beginning, was to pay writers. We're very proud of the fact we don't publish unpaid journalism and we don't use unpaid interns." They have added fundraising capacity to go after grants.

While theirs is a decidedly grassroots effort, being lean doesn't equate to a lack of impact. Cox said, "I've recently been doing deep research into the relative online success of various outlets by comparing publicly available share data from Facebook. Shockingly, or not, the legacy outlets are at the bottom of the heap for online traffic. Outside of the occasional viral hit, newspapers like the *Globe*, *Gazette* and *La Presse* get negligible traffic on much of the content they post. We're beating them in traffic per piece, but I imagine so are the *Tyee* and other outlets that are a bit more digital native. The big winners are clickbait and partial clickbait outlets like Buzzfeed and Vice, followed by outlets like Ricochet and the *Tyee*, and at the very bottom are the legacy outlets. They're totally dysfunctional at promoting content through social media, and it's killing them."[41]

Ricochet is notable for its explicit recognition of the growing importance of Aboriginal voices in Canada through its division of content into four main sections: Canada, Quebec, Indigenous, and International.[42] Against a lot of competing alternatives in English, Cox said Ricochet holds its own, but its French edition "is the first and remains the only daily independent media outlet in Quebec." And, like any self-respecting agitprop venture, Ricochet derives much of its satisfaction from the degree to which it challenges convention. "We're routinely attacked in the pages of the *Journal de Montreal*, a tabloid with the largest print circulation in the province, where we've been described with frustration as the 'Rolls Royce of progressive media' and another colourful idiom that translates loosely to 'those smart ass young people who are good at technology.'"

What many of these initiatives have in common is their progressive tilt, their ties to social movements, and, sadly, their failure to grow beyond being small, plucky operations that battle the financial odds rather than getting to play them. But for all that, there's something they do much better than mainstream media—which is irritate the hell out of people, especially those in government and industry who are bent on maintaining the status quo. Out west, a particular target of the *Observer* and the *Tyee* is the oil and gas sector. So concerned is this industry about the influence of these relatively small players that *Alberta Oil* magazine ran a lengthy feature in early 2016 in which it characterized their work as constituting a "Vancouver School" of activist journalism that industry ignores at its peril.[43] "Together with lesser known and more dubious websites like the *Commonsense Canadian* and *West Coast Native News,* the *Observer* and the *Tyee* are part of an emerging Vancouver School of media that is challenging traditional journalism and finding a ready audience among eco-activist readers. More importantly, their influence is starting to spread beyond the borders of the Lower Mainland, and rallying Canadians against energy infrastructure projects outside B.C., such as the $15.7-billion Energy East pipeline." The notion of a "Vancouver School" of journalism disrupting Canada's polluters-in-chief has an ironic ring to it, coming from an oil patch that has been crafted more along the lines of the Chicago School of economics.

But if the Vancouver School has been good at questioning the business practices of some of the biggest companies in the land, it has done less well at monetizing that work. Even less successful in Canada have been commercial attempts to launch new web entities that make a virtue of well-reported public-interest journalism. Flame-outs in that category include the Mark News and OpenFile. One survivor is iPolitics[44]—backed by private investors and still afloat after several years. The *Tyee,* meanwhile,[45] is hardly robustly funded but has seen success in diversifying its revenue sources and becoming less reliant over time on initial investors. It has patient investment from Working Enterprises, a labour-affiliated fund, and Eric Peterson and Christina Munck, a couple heavily involved in philanthropic enterprises on BC's coast through their private

Tula Foundation. Together these two investors underwrite slightly less than half of the *Tyee*'s operational needs. The other half of the *Tyee*'s growing budget is supported by diverse earned revenues: crowd-funded contributions from readers and organizations, advertising, event sponsorships, and master classes offering an array of professional development opportunities. A sister organization—the Tyee Solutions Society—has separately funded larger public-interest journalism projects that the *Tyee* and other media outlets publish. The *Tyee* was singled out in "Survival Strategies for Local Journalism," a 2015 story in the *New Yorker*, for its "model of diversification" as a route to sustainability.[46] The *Vancouver Observer* has also had some success with crowd-funding, as has a terrific online terrier focused on climate policy, the BC-based *DeSmogBlog*.

None of these genesis stories for independent news websites quite fit the common experience south of the border. Recent studies by the Pew Research Center[47] and the Knight Foundation[48] looked at the dozens of non-profit experiments underway in the US, finding them "fragile" and mostly dependent on philanthropy.[49] Most were started with money from foundations or wealthy individuals and continue to rely on substantial philanthropic infusions as they strive to diversify their revenue streams. But at least the US has a large and healthy philanthropic sector with a long tradition of funding alternative media such as *Mother Jones, Harper's*, the *Nation*, the *New Republic, Alternet*, and ProPublica.

ONE CANADIAN, PURELY philanthropically funded model
that has shown promise is the Tyee Solutions Society (TSS).
It was created in 2009 as a non-profit sister organization to
the *Tyee*'s (to date profitless) for-profit model.[50] TSS projects are almost entirely charitably funded and (like much
of ProPublica's work) shared with other media outlets without charge. They are necessarily focused on solutions rather
than muckraking because Canada's tax laws restrict charities to expending no more than 10 per cent of their dollars
funding "political activities," and the law is vague enough
that almost any hard-hitting journalism that holds political entities accountable falls under that category. In fact,
TSS pioneered solutions journalism in North America (the
Solutions Journalism Network was launched in 2013—a
rare instance of a US media innovation, albeit headed by a
Canadian, following on the heels of a Canadian one).

Other charitably supported journalistic endeavours
include the Toronto-based Journalists for Human Rights;
another is the *Walrus* magazine. But it simply isn't possible, anywhere in Canada, to point to a non-profit or even
a blended-value journalism enterprise that has achieved
scale either in audience terms, business terms, or as a
serious disruptor to the media status quo. It doesn't help
that Canada's philanthropic laws, unlike those in the US,
make it very difficult for foundations to fund journalism
that might be interpreted as politically partisan. This has
served to restrict philanthropic funding for Canadian journalism to just a trickle. As for the capital markets, there

hasn't been much evidence that venture capital or even so-called impact investments are readily available to fund media disruptors, either.

This creates a double whammy against would-be Canadian media entrepreneurs. In the US, a wave of investment has poured into digital media, new and not so new.[51] Examples range from First Look Media[52] (the eBay founder's start-up that includes Glenn Greenwald's *Intercept*); the aforementioned ProPublica;[53] *Vox*,[54] part of a $140 million USD company headed by former *Washington Post* data-mapping journalist star Ezra Klein that draws millions to its smart breakdowns with a promise to "Explain the news"; and Amazon.com founder Jeff Bezos's $250 million USD purchase[55] of the *Washington Post*. This relative media gold rush is fuelled by a number of factors: wellsprings of venture capital in search of opportunities, large audiences and marketing industries, a legacy of media diversity and innovation, and opportunities for encouraging and developing journalistic talent. None of these factors apply in Canada.

FOUR

Whither the Future?

COMING OFF SEVERAL months of reading about, conducting interviews about, sampling different products from, and travelling across and beyond the borders of Canada's contemporary media landscape, it is clear there are no simple remedies for what ails Canadian media. Its afflictions are part of a massive and continuing disruption of global media, made all the more challenging by our enormous service area—much of it sparsely populated, a relatively small population, anemic local revenue models, enormous competition from behemoth social-media brands, high levels of ownership concentration, too *little* competition around quality content production, and a stubborn unwillingness of legacy media to leave the stage.

I have separated my concluding thoughts into two fields, one focused on philanthropy's potential role, the other casting more widely to contemplate what the marketplace might yield in the years to come. In both instances, there are roles for governments, too.

Philanthropy: Putting its money where its mouth wants to be

WHEN I LEFT the CBC in 1994 to become the founding executive director of Ecotrust Canada, a constant refrain I heard in the environmental-NGO community was that *the environment* never got the attention it deserved in the media, which meant the political elites paid less attention than they might and that during elections, even if environmental issues had at times been on the front pages or at the top of newscasts, *the economy* always jumped back to the top of the list of public concerns. The environment inevitably slid down that list, and elections were won or lost over who could most convincingly claim to have a political agenda that was going to be "good for the economy," based mostly on projections about economic growth and job creation.

I'm sure other "special interests" feel the same way as environmentalists when they see the economy reified in the public realm as something incarnate, something that might *suffer* if not properly tended to, while real human suffering is deemed acceptable as the price of keeping our economy "healthy." Thus it is that BC premier Christy Clark, for example, can be lauded[1] for taking a "prudent, disciplined approach" to managing the provincial treasury while BC's kids are among the poorest in the land[2] and an unconscionable number of children, half of them Aboriginal, are apprehended by the state[3] in numbers that exceed those caught up in the dark era of residential schools.[4] It's really no different in other provinces, or at the federal level. We are constantly fed a line that economic growth is good, ipso facto, and that without it we will all shiver our way into impoverishment. Very occasionally, there is a faint dissenting voice from the One Percent, as when Vancouver mining magnate Ross Beaty attacked "the pursuit of continuous growth [as] the bedrock economic model of our time. Outdated and unsustainable, it is still advocated, recklessly and relentlessly, by federal, provincial and nearly all municipal governments."[5]

This incessant echo about the need for economic growth is the meta-narrative that has shaped the contours of the developed world's behaviour since the birth of the first baby boomer. It is how, perversely, so many governments are able to gain and maintain power by preaching "economic austerity" as a virtue. "But our economic constraints are also coupled with an austerity of imagination, an austerity of hope for the future," says one of Canada's leading thinkers in the field of social innovation, Ric Young.[6] And it is that hope for the future, or those joint and several hopes for the future, that continues to founder in the wistful shallows of do-goodism, while the economic determinists swim in the deep end and get to decide not just the temperature of the water, but of the atmosphere, too.

The industry of philanthropy, meanwhile—whether an honest modern-day articulation of the Greeks' *philanthrōpía*, or love for humankind, or a sort of post-colonial and pre-apocalyptic triage system for assuaging capitalist guilt and earning some tax concessions en route—has long exhibited an abundance of hope for the future but an austerity of imagination or capacity for actually achieving it. Charitable foundations, like the NGOs and environmental NGOs they support, continue to sit mostly at the sidelines of decision-making because they, and their issues, remain mostly peripheral to the dominant narrative of generations since the end of World War II. In Canada, at least in part, that's because there has been no coherent, sustained, and collaborative approach to building an alternative narrative of the country. The sum of all our good intentions thus appears as a rounding error on our national accounts, even as the language of philanthropy is littered with words like impact, leverage, innovation, transformation, and scale.

If changing our "bedrock economic model" is essential to achieving breakthroughs in social innovation—and how can it not be?—then it stands to reason that we need an entirely new meta-narrative for our times. A sliver of this emerged in late 2015 at the COP21 talks in Paris, where, finally, the environment *was* given the attention it deserved, even if the climate talks still resound with the logic of what is "affordable" and "achievable" within economic constraints that are, of course, going to be meaningless if our economies drown when the oceans rise. No matter, the point is that there is now a huge opportunity to disrupt everything, and in the case of our national media, that's like blowing on a house made of straw. Our media are disrupting themselves. The question is, does philanthropy have the courage of its own convictions to plant the seedbed of a new, progressive narrative for Canada? If ours is *No Country for Old Media*, with apologies to Cormac McCarthy, then how do we avoid going down *The Road* to a bleak, wreckage-strewn media landscape dimly lit by the fires of good intentions? It is simply not enough to hope to get a few more "positive" stories placed into the *Globe*, or even, laudable as it is, to sponsor a couple of progressive "beat" reporters at the *Star,* as have both the Atkinson Foundation[7] and Tides Canada.[8] The media economy is currently so unstable that it is hard to imagine more perfect conditions in which philanthropies could direct some of that disruption to their own ends and, more importantly, to the benefit of the communities they purport to serve— after first having earned their tax relief.

The immediate—and dare I say *Canadian*—rejoinder to that might be that, well, Canadian foundations are small, certainly by comparison to their American cousins. True that. If Canadian foundations do seek to have influence and to have a positive impact in emerging media, they are likely to do so vicariously, rather than assuming outright ownership of new or existing media properties (although this does not rule out the potential impact of investing in new media if and when appropriate). Partnerships and collaborations are key, since foundations are likely more inclined towards building an ecosystem for progressive media impact in Canada, rather than becoming the sole source for it, or seeking a single solution to what ails the field. Impact is essential (otherwise why bother?), but that is no small consideration given the size of the industry and the relative modesty of available resources. "Acupuncture philanthropy," in the words of Rockefeller Brothers Fund president Stephen Heintz,[9] would seem to be what's most achievable—skillfully administered interventions for cata- lytic effects, perhaps executed under the auspices of some kind of media-impact funder collaborative. Already in Canada there are coalitions of environmental grant mak- ers (Canadian Environmental Grantmakers' Network); an Aboriginal-focused one (the Circle on Philanthropy and Aboriginal Peoples in Canada); there's an early child- hood development funders' working group; plus, there are foundation networks such as Philanthropic Foundations Canada, and Community Foundations of Canada.

Whether a media innovation funder collaborative would enable and/or leverage investments in new media or just promote earnest dialogue is a question worth answering before another organization is worth launching.

Certainly, since the McCarthyesque days of the Harper regime, there is a certain flush of hope in the charitable sec- tor that the Canada Revenue Agency's witch hunt against, especially, environmental NGOs as a result of their tar sands advocacy is now at an end. Even before Harper,

Canada's charities law did not exactly invite behaviour that encourages advocacy, without which efforts to influence public opinion and create normative (and policy) shifts in public discourse, policy, and behaviour have come to seem like mere feints in the ring. Nor, as mentioned earlier, do our tax laws favour charitable investments in media. As John Stackhouse writes,[10] "U.S. tax laws allow foundations, companies and individuals to donate to an entity that publishes a newspaper, as long as their messages are not construed as trying to sell something. Canadian laws could be restructured to better enable more efforts like the foundation that finances *Walrus* magazine, to support commercially oriented, journalistically driven digital news operations."

Jonathan Kay, editor of the *Walrus*, once edited the fiendishly pro-business editorial pages of the *National Post*, but even he allows that "the free market can no longer guarantee the survival of high quality journalism."[11] Then again, the *Walrus*—a flaccid, self-satisfied kind of poor man's *New Yorker*—hardly qualifies as the standard-bearer for great journalism that Kay claims it is. Its "commercial orientation" has led it to an ignoble bedfellowship with Enbridge, and if *Canadaland* is any guide,[12] the magazine's alleged failure to meet its obligations in observing Canada's charity laws don't exactly make it a poster child for grant-supported journalism either. But the *Walrus* aside, Stackhouse's point is a good one. "Such [tax] alternatives might encourage owners to stay away from the stock market, an investment model that is not suited at the moment to the journalism business" because the profits and cash flow of years past have been replaced by marginal profits, longer timelines, and greater risks more suited to "patient capital" of the Graeme Wood kind.

Assuming the conditions necessary for granting to or investing in new-generation media improve, or at least don't get any worse, how might philanthropy go about doing that? As referenced above, a collaboration between funders might be one way to aggregate enough resources to make it worth doing. Maybe Canada, which once prided itself on solution-finding (universal health care, international peacekeeping, Céline Dion), could become a world leader in solutions journalism, taking its cue and learning some lessons from more than $750,000 worth of Tyee Solutions Society projects already funded and published. David Beers, founding editor of the *Tyee* and of its solutions society, says "Philanthropies interested in helping to strengthen and diversify Canada's news media may want to begin with the aims in their charters, and then think strategically about how to make the impact in keeping with those aims."[13] He kindly provided a selective taxonomy of new media initiatives for reference in Table 1.

TABLE 1. Funding targets for philanthropies that want to strengthen and diversify Canada's news media. (David Beers)

FUNDING TARGET	TARGET'S TRAITS	TYPE OF SUPPORTS	POTENTIAL IMPACT	EXAMPLES
Individual journalists, media workers	Freelance or staff journalists seeking to expand their skills, explore an issue or topic, make a living	Underwrite scholarships, fellowships, awards, positions, or beats	New wave of reporters trained, new content created, media organizational capacity expanded	Atkinson fellowships; Canadian Journalism Foundation fellowships
Publications	New or existing electronic and/or print publications that attract loyal audiences sharing values, interests	Seed money or grants for business or content development, core funding, or special projects	Audience communities built, media sources diversified, bases built for journalists to operate from	*Tyee*, *Walrus*, *Vancouver Observer*, Ricochet, iPolitics
Content generators	New or existing organizations that create research, articles, video, etc., to share with media outlets	Seed money or grants for business or content development, core funding, or special projects	New reporting about desired topics, existing media leveraged to reach wide audiences	Journalists for Human Rights, Tyee Solutions Society
Multi-partner projects	Collaborative and multi-faceted projects that produce content, train reporters in solutions journalism	Help frame, fund an initiative, promote collaboration among organizations to make it happen	Creative relations among organizations built, their capacities broadened, content made and/or published	Leading Together: Indigenous Youth in Community Partnerships (McConnell Foundation), Discourse Media
Innovation incubators	New media experiments in tech, social design, business models	Competitions for grants, creative summits, venture capital investing, documenting best practices	Tech and social innovation harnessed to aid public interest media amidst market failure	Knight News Challenge, Mozilla Project
Higher education	Research, teaching, logistics, and equipment for academics and students	Grants, fellowships	New wave of reporters trained in desired methods, values, focuses. More media research, experimentation	International Reporting Program (UBC); Reporting in Indigenous Communities (UBC); Munk School fellowships (U of T)
Media policy	Researchers, advocates aiming to reform anti-democratic elements of the mediasphere	Grants, research, advocacy gatherings, lobbying	Obstacles to new media reduced, ownership de-concentrated, funding options for charities legally expanded	Media Reform Coalition (UK), Media Democracy Project, OpenMedia

In the meantime, Joshua Benton at Nieman Lab is keen to convene Canadian philanthropic players around what can be learned from the ample experience south of the border, in terms of process and practice, to help obviate a lot of tail-chasing by Canadian foundations new to this domain. Perhaps philanthropic collaborations could straddle the border, for instance with the Knight Foundation creating a Canadian media-innovation "inbox" for promising start-ups that Canadian foundations could efficiently road-test. In our post–Truth and Reconciliation Commission era, Canadian foundations could introduce a conscious selection bias towards local and Aboriginal journalism innovations, and possibly learn from and encourage something akin to the Van Jones initiative to get low-opportunity youth into coding—potentially in conjunction with universities or trade schools.

RICOCHET ESTIMATES THAT "fewer than two dozen full-time journalists cover an Indigenous beat."[14] This in a country with 630 Aboriginal communities and an indigenous population of 1.4 million. That's 0.17 per cent of Canada's 14,000 journalists covering a population comprising 4 per cent of Canadians—arguably a population segment that needs the services of journalists more than any other. That's a per capita shortfall of more than 500 journalists right there. A study by Policy Options released in May 2016 suggested that "rebalancing the relationship between Canada's Indigenous peoples and the rest of the

population is one of the most difficult public policy challenges of our time. Reconciliation will involve many costly
and difficult public policy initiatives. The level of public support necessary will require a journalism that goes
beyond crisis reporting to challenge the long held images
and stereotypes of Indigenous peoples and probe more
deeply into the root causes of despair in First Nations."[15]
The study's assessment of the status quo does not make for
pleasant reading, citing mainstream media's "institutional
lack of interest" in indigenous issues and "significant gaps
and distortions" in the coverage that does take place "when
there are so few journalists who have in-depth knowledge
of Indigenous communities, values and cultures. Given the
importance of reconciliation, this is counterproductive,
and it is largely correctable." That's something a consor-
tium of funders could help address, because mainstream
media showed precious little leadership in this space even
before their business models began to implode.

In fact, diversity—indigenous or otherwise—is missing in most Canadian media, although it is only *reported*
missing by the likes of *Canadaland*. In March 2016, *Canadaland* revealed that only 3 of 18 newspapers it contacted
filled out a survey with questions that included, "How
many full-time staff do you employ in your newsroom?"
and "How many full-time staff identify as Aboriginal?"[16]
It was a careful, politely worded survey that guaranteed
anonymity. It asked for statistical data on the racial and
ethnic makeup of our country's largest newsrooms in order

to "understand the attitudes about diversity held by news-papers. The survey asked whether those filling it out, be it the HR department or the editor-in-chief, would be will-ing to be interviewed about diversity in their newsrooms. None were."

In its account, *Canadaland* quoted Margo Goodhand, late of the *Winnipeg Free Press* and the *Edmonton Journal*, who said editors were eager to address issues of diversity: "Every editor that I ever worked with cared deeply about it." During Goodhand's time at the *Free Press*, the paper launched the John W. Dafoe scholarship for Aboriginal students. "You desperately wanted to have an Aboriginal journalist and it just didn't happen," she said. "First of all there weren't very many coming out of the colleges, and the ones that did said why would they want to work in a main-stream newspaper?" She found most young indigenous reporters wanted to work in broadcast at either the CBC or APTN (the Aboriginal Peoples Television Network). For Goodhand, the strangulation of print media's economic viability, not the willingness of its front-line editors, is the biggest obstacle for papers that might want to hire non-white staff. "Traditional media [have] so many other things they're worrying about, like surviving, they just go, 'That's one of those things we wish we could do.'" But mostly they don't. Goodhand later told me, "We need more indigenous journalism, desperately."[17]

Jesse Brown convened an indigenous media round table on *Canadaland* in February 2016,[18] featuring a wonderfully diverse group of panelists: Maureen Googoo, owner and editor of Kukukwes, a news website covering indigenous news in Atlantic Canada; Leena Minifie, the editor of Ricochet's Indigenous Reporting Fund; Jarrett Martineau, co-founder and creative producer for Revolutions Per Minute, a music platform dedicated to discovering indigenous culture, and a producer for VICELAND; Ryan McMahon, creator of *Red Man Laughing,* a comedy podcast, and founder of *Indian & Cowboy,* the world's only listener-supported indigenous podcast network; and Waubgeshig Rice, a video journalist with CBC Ottawa. They provided understandable laments for how profoundly indigenous communities are underserved by mainstream media, mixed with heartening insights into how well some independent media sites are doing at overcoming barriers and getting the job done themselves. Philanthropists could do a lot worse things with their time than spending 41 minutes and 25 seconds listening to *Canadaland* Episode #120. They might also want to look in on the Quebec-based mobile filmmaking studio Wapikoni,[19] which is doing pioneering work helping indigenous youth learn to use digital tools in their storytelling.

ONE OTHER CONSIDERATION for foundations is what to do with their own learnings, given the poor job of dissemination that most foundations currently do. It certainly seems that foundations fund an enormous amount of research and support sometimes remarkable experiments, or "proofs of possibilities," to use Ric Young's phrase, that never make it outside the beltway. As the *Washington Post* rather mischievously put it, "What if someone had already figured out the answers to the world's most pressing policy problems, but those solutions were buried deep in a PDF, somewhere nobody will ever read them?"[20] The World Bank, the report said, is one of those "high-minded organizations" that release hundreds if not thousands of reports every year. "The World Bank recently decided to ask an important question: *Is anyone actually reading these things?* They dug into their Web site traffic data and came to the following conclusions: Nearly one-third of their PDF reports had never been downloaded, not even once. Another 40 per cent of their reports had been downloaded fewer than 100 times. Only 13 percent had seen more than 250 downloads in their lifetimes. Since most World Bank reports have a stated objective of informing public debate or government policy, this seems like a pretty lousy track record."

As Shefa Siegel suggests in relation to international development,[21] a "pestilence of paper has plagued internationalism from its inception. Over the nine weeks of the UN's founding conference in San Francisco, participants consumed seventy-eight tons—a half-million sheets—of paper *per day*, propelling a fetish that led Canada's Lester Pearson, an early leader of the United Nations, to describe that organization in 1970 as 'drowning in its own words and suffocating in its own documents.'" The point is, who among Canada's foundations is not guilty of the same? The

Vancouver Foundation is to be congratulated on announcing[22] in 2015 its commitment to an "open licensing policy for projects funded through its community granting programs. The foundation's goal is to advance transparency and accessibility of materials to drive greater innovation and creativity in British Columbia and beyond," starting in 2017. But as helpful as this might be, more dissemination of what foundations and their partners are learning out in the world doesn't necessarily equate with *better* dissemination. It might just move the burden of drowning and suffocating from inside a foundation to outside it.

To fully take advantage of the disruptions of the digital age, foundations could in effect create their own newsrooms, especially when it comes to feeding ideas into the pool for solutions journalism. Robert Steiner at the Munk School has done plenty of thinking about how non-profits can benefit from the current media revolution,[23] suggesting that "non-profits that know how to help news media cover a public issue—and who can undertake those collaborations responsibly—are now in a better position than ever to engage the public." The same would seem to hold for foundations. At the very least, as part of their grant-making requirements, they could train, or cajole, or insist upon their grantees acting much as Steiner recommends, which means becoming great reporters about the issues they know the most about.

There are doubtless other ways in which foundations can move the media needle, and undoubtedly their trustees will want to know if any of it makes a difference. In addition to the aforementioned Media Impact Funders, it is worth taking into consideration the findings on measuring media impact that were reported in the fall of 2015 in the *Stanford Social Innovation Review*.[24] "Donors are seeking ways to measure the impact of the media projects that they fund, and media organizations in turn are working to track the real-world effects of what they publish—partly in the hope that proving their worth will help enable their survival," the paper said. "All around the world, media outlets are learning that some funders are uncomfortable with supporting journalism merely as a 'public good.' They want to see proof of impact." The authors cite one (unnamed) grant maker who worries about a growing "impact-industrial complex" in which an obsession with measuring impact displaces work that might actually achieve it. They also caution that if newsrooms tailor reporting "to stories that can have immediate effects or quantifiable results, they might be unwilling to cover large, persistent—yet vitally important—social problems. Ultimately, the impact that journalists can have on society will erode if they must serve the whims of funders. That is true whether the funders in question are government officials, advertisers, corporate owners, or well-intentioned philanthropists."

Finally, skeptical foundation executives or trustees might wonder whether any amount they invest in Canadian media will add up to more than a spit in our three oceans, and more to the point, whether the country will be any better for it. One could justifiably point out that in the US, where support for independent journalism is strong and growing, the Koch brothers' influence and impact is no less pernicious, Sheldon Adelson is no less the Republican kingmaker, and the National Rifle Association still co-signs the death certificates of 30,000 Americans a year and even has its own radio station![25] As for Donald Trump... well, maybe in an aberrant 2016, Adelson *is* less the Republican kingmaker, but you get the idea.

America hasn't become more like Canada because it has NPR and the *New York Times*, Bernie Sanders notwithstanding. American television is, as Hunter S. Thompson once said, a "cruel and shallow money trench through the heart of the journalism industry, a long plastic hallway where thieves and pimps run free and good men die like dogs, for no good reason."[26] Or at least Fox News is. And here's the thing: "When it comes to getting news about politics and government, liberals and conservatives inhabit different worlds," the Pew Research Center found.[27] Conservatives "are tightly clustered around a single news source... with 47% citing Fox News as their main source for news about government and politics." Lily-livered liberals (my term, not Pew's) cluster... well, the point is they don't. They split their time between NPR and the *Times* and CNN and MSNBC, and no doubt they put in plenty of time on social, as well. But the reality is, the American right has its bought-and-paid-for think-tanks that feed its bought-and-paid-for media with daily distortions that make the news cycle look like an outtake from *Mad Max*. And let's face it, there are plenty of Canadians who dial in to shock jocks and ranters, read *Sun* newspapers and transit freebies, and think Stephen Harper had it just right when he eschewed established media channels in favour of talking to "grassroots" journalists.

So, would investments in more liberal, solutions-based, service-oriented, narrative-altering media in Canada make a difference? Sure they would. Under Harper, Canada came dangerously close to becoming a lot more like America, and not in a good way. The ground for media disruption in this country has already been tilled. The opportunity to buy a lifetime pass to a whole different media game has probably never been more tantalizingly within reach in Canada, nor the need more urgent. Which makes my own thinking about philanthropy, private capital, and government's potential roles in seizing the media moment here seem too prototypically Canadian, too tepid—my thoughts shot through with caveats that we don't have the money, our entrepreneurs won't be bold enough, our governments have too many other things to worry about.

So let me end this section by framing what some combination of foundation, private, and public capital might achieve in this space on a slightly different, bolder note. Why not a Canadian ProPublica? Why not a Canadian Graeme Wood stepping up and saying, "Twenty million clams? Sure. Let's get the *Guardian* over here and raise hell!" Why not a crowd-funded equivalent of

De Correspondent? Why not a Canadian version of Nieman Lab or a Canadian "inbox" at the Knight Foundation? Why not a campaign to have all the money that's been earmarked to send back to the CBC sent to APTN instead? That could help reconcile a few things right there. Why not, in sum, a serious investment in Canada in producing what Mathias Döpfner of Axel Springer dreams of, which is digital journalism that "should be and could be" better than anything we've ever seen in print?

New media: Only game-changers need apply

"IN 2013, VENTURE capital firms—the William Randolph Hearsts of today—invested more than $300 million in new media,"[28] wrote John Stackhouse in *Mass Disruption*. Of course, he was writing about the US, not Canada. Also in the US, "a group of concerned citizens came together in 2009 to launch the *Texas Tribune*, a non-partisan, online newspaper focused on state politics."[29] They raised $27 million USD, and the *Texas Tribune* has become one of the most celebrated new media start-ups in the country. Stackhouse writes: "As its editor, CEO and co-founder Evan Smith told me, anyone in government or public life who is interested in anything serious about Texas comes first to the *Tribune*." In a conversation[30] soon after the release of his book, Stackhouse told me that for his money (which it isn't), the *Texas Tribune* is a model of what a non-profit, essentially blended-value (my term, not his) news operation can look like in the new media age. It also goes some distance towards addressing one of the biggest concerns arising from the digital revolution, which is what happens to local news. After all, "All politics is local," former speaker of the US House of Representatives Tip O'Neill once famously said.[31] And yet there is less and less local news, or conversely, a growing "news poverty" here in Canada, as Ryerson's April Lindgren has found. This seems to me to be the kind of nation-building arena in which the federal government could and should play a big part.

Many Canadians will remember a time when good-quality Australian films seemed to pop up with great regularity. They came about in the 1980s because of tax incentives for Australian-made film and television productions, whose investors were allowed a 150 per cent tax concession on their investment at risk.[32] When the tax concessions were reined in, the production and distribution of Australian films dropped dramatically and has never really recovered—when did you last see a great Australian film?

Closer to home, Vancouver—or Hollywood North, as it has come to be known—became a location of choice in part because of the often advantageous exchange rate for American film producers, but also because of a production tax credit that cost the province $343 million in 2014–15 but underpinned an industry worth $2 billion that same year.[33] Elsewhere, such as in Saskatchewan and Nova Scotia, cancellation of film tax credits has decimated the industry and led to steep job losses. The fact is that tax credits work for film, and there's no reason they couldn't work for other media, too.

Interestingly, there seems to be little hunger in Canada for any sort of government bailout of ailing media. "Some media critics have called on the federal government to step in and give the country's newspapers financial assistance that could get them through the next few years," the Canadian Press wrote in January 2016.[34] At least Paul Godfrey, whose Postmedia could use help more than most, had the good grace to say he's not interested in asking for the government's help. "As far as I'm concerned I'm running a business right now," he said. "The preferential route is to explore all options we can do by ourselves first." Madelaine Drohan writes that part of the general reluctance to countenance government support is "the potential for state interference in a free press" that would come about through direct government subsidy of private media outlets.[35] Sylvia Stead, public editor of the *Globe and Mail,* asked out loud when Hedy Fry launched her Commons committee inquiry, "Is state intervention the answer, or even likely?... What levers does the government even have to save something like local news?... On what basis could the committee now recommend financial support to some media and not to others?"[36] Paul Watson, meanwhile, told me, "It's nauseating to hear journalists, especially veterans of the business, hoping aloud for government support. That would only prop up the problem. And journalists ought to be ashamed to seek help from the very politicians and bureaucrats we are supposed to be holding to account. The smart way forward is to let failed legacy media die natural deaths and support the brave, hard-working start-ups and independents who are building the future."[37]

Phillip Smith, speaking from the audience at a Vancouver Press Club panel on the future of journalism in April 2016, basically invoked Nike (the shoe company, not the winged goddess of victory) when he argued that we should just do it, "it" being rebuilding Canadian journalism without waiting around for a helping hand. Smith, who among other things is director of technology at the *Tyee*, alternates between "inspiration and desperation" when he surveys Canadian media. Canada and its media have become "increasingly irrelevant in a world of countries that are trying to actually innovate," he wrote in *Medium*.[38] "Increasingly a follower, instead of a trail-blazer, Canada's biggest journalism export is quickly becoming its talent—smart people who see better opportunities elsewhere." Yet Smith finds sufficient opportunity in the scrapyard of Canadian media to build something new, "to re-direct the conversation away from 'How to save Canada's media,' and toward questions of how to radically re-invent a media ecosystem that puts Canada back on the global stage—an exportable model; a desirable product beyond Canada's borders; an inspiration to the world."

Smith cites "a handful" of Canadian experiments that show promise. "For better or worse, Vice Media demonstrates a forward-thinking media product that is both

uniquely Canadian and also *desirable* beyond our borders—and it is now a rapidly-expanding global platform.
Outside of the publishing world, media technology companies like Hootsuite and ScribbleLive immediately come
to mind—both saw underserved opportunities, quickly
moved to solve them, and now export their products
around the globe. What makes... Vice, Hootsuite, and
ScribbleLive different in my mind is their relentless entre-
preneurial focus and global ambitions. They make Canada
look 'cool,' while also understanding a critical reality: there
is no 'Canadian market' anymore. In an era of fast, affordable, ubiquitous Internet access and inexpensive shipping,
all markets are global."

Smith is the first to admit that technology companies
are not synonymous with journalism providers—Hootsuite
and ScribbleLive are marketers, and VICE only partly suc-
ceeds in drawing a line between lurid entertainment and
serious journalism—but he thinks two Canadian start-ups
worth watching are I Fucking Love Science[39] and Diply.[40]
At the Press Club event in Vancouver, Smith urged us to
suspend disbelief about their journalistic merits—they
seem to have none—and focus instead on how brilliantly
they have found audiences. In a note to me after the event,
he wrote:

Both are exemplary of the current best practices for a
media undertaking in 2016: they go to where the audience is (social networks) and give that audience what it

wants (short, autoplay, captioned video and attention-capturing curated links). Their content is platform agnostic, highly shareable, and mobile first. They both have grown huge audiences (IFLS, 24 million Facebook fans; Diply.com, 150 million monthly unique visitors)... Are these two undertakings examples of the "future of journalism"? I do not know. What I do know is that they've grown audiences that far exceed many traditional news media in Canada, and that even small efforts at "informing, not just entertaining" would reach huge numbers of people. More than that, the revenue—and future potential revenue—that these two experiments are demonstrating would fund a lot of reporting.

Of course, there is no guarantee that's where their owners will take them, although who ever imagined that VICE would leverage its sophomoric ribaldry into a global media brand that aspires to be taken seriously? Smith's invocations to think very differently about pathways to new journalism are refreshing, and add further fuel to Watson's contention that failed legacy media should go gentle into that good night, and independents should bootstrap the future.

But I still think there is a role for government. There is a distinction to be made between propping up deadwood newspapers—don't bother—and supporting the technical development and product initiation of quality digital platforms upon which journalists—themselves unsubsidized by the government—can practise their craft. This is an area where an interventionist federal government could play a role in Canada—providing incentives to accelerate a faster and more fulsome entry into a digital revolution that is fast spinning beyond Canada's grasp, unless you fucking love science. "A subsidy!" goes the neo-liberal cry. Sure, maybe paid for by a clawback from the subsidies that the federal government hands out to the oil industry—variously pegged at $34 billion a year[41] or $1.7 billion a year,[42] depending on whether you read the *Tyee* or the *Globe and Mail*. Which is either a lot of money or 20 times a lot of money being spent on a dinosaur instead of a phoenix.

In early 2016, the CRTC began hearings about the future of local television,[43] in part to consider whether to restore the Local Programming Improvement Fund to subsidize local news. But why restrict such a fund to television, and why only within the confined mandate of the CRTC? Some kind of media improvement fund could be established to help promote innovation and scaling across *all* media platforms in Canada—or at least all digital ones. Mme Joly?

And while the Heritage Minister is seeking succour from Finance and the Treasury Board for tax incentives for investments in emerging media, she might also apply her department to the urgent task of doing a root-and-branch rethink of the CBC's mandate: its relationship with government, its governance, its long-term funding model, its embrace of more agile technologies, its willingness to

consider more innovative content and distribution partnerships, and its role as a national service. As Konrad
Yakabuski says, "If giving the public broadcaster an extra
$150-million merely allows it to go back to what it was
doing before the Tories came to town, [Joly] will only be
postponing its demise."[44] The minister might also want to
encourage the CBC to contemplate a name change, since a
modern country doesn't need a "broadcasting corporation"
so much as a *storytelling service*. If the CBC cannot retool
accordingly, why not spend the money instead on helping
remote communities get online, so they can tell stories
to themselves? "Is high-speed Internet a basic right?" a
Globe and Mail headline asked in April 2016, and it is a
very good question.[45] Just as the Inuit claim the right to
be cold as a fundamental human right,[46] isn't access to
storytelling and story *sharing* technology a basic human
right for indigenous peoples in Canada? We tore that away
with residential schools. The least we can do is give it back,
adjusted for technology.

The best story wins

IN THE END, what a more innovative, inclusive, sustainable, and resilient society needs most of all is a good story.
Or 35 million of them, told to each other every day in the
most inventive, inclusive, instructive, and inspiring ways
we can stoop to conjure. A few years ago, Ric Young talked
about the importance of story to an audience in Markham,

Ontario.[47] To the researchers who helped him prepare for his speech,

> I set the question: can a city be a genius?... And we found story after story of places that are breaking through. It's not the conventional narrative. Normally we hear the stories that are problem-focused—stories of despair, dysfunction, disenfranchisement. The story that's all loaded up with data about the problem, that's entirely focused on what's wrong. I think it's a debilitating story. A story that dampens our spirit, and limits our imagination... and our courage. The more we tell that story, the more we convince ourselves that we are stuck. But we are not stuck. Big change is possible. A city can be a genius.

To which I would add, a country can, too—and maybe even a *sector* within a country that is part and parcel of what makes a good country better. For all the sorry state of our media, Canada's genius media moment might just be now. The art might be less in trying to engineer new media technologies, but rather in formulating not just for ourselves, but for the world, a new narrative that privileges personal and community growth over economic growth—a narrative that is utterly disruptive to the status quo. A narrative that, if powerful enough, will find its way onto whatever platforms there are to mobilize it in the public sphere.

The very idea of a "disruptive narrative" is one we owe to Ric Young, who says,[48]

The ability to frame and champion a compelling narrative is central to the work of transformational leadership. Great leaders are first and foremost creators of stories that can galvanize others—stories that can invest distant and challenging goals with meaning and appeal. Recent research in neuroscience has shown how human beings are hard-wired for stories. We have story-patterning brains, both constructing and attending to meaning in narrative form. But even without the brain-mapping confirmation of this, the powerful force of stories is evident throughout cultures and throughout history.

Compelling stories capture our imagination, engage us emotionally, and move us. Narrative logic is not the same as factual logic. There is little room for moral appeal in a business case that builds a rational argument around a value proposition. But there is no compelling story—or convincing call to purpose—in a narrative that does not appeal in some way to our moral sensibilities. In fictional stories we are drawn into the challenge faced by the characters. In the stories transformative leaders craft, we are drawn into the challenges we collectively face. As George Akerlof says, "The confidence of a nation, or of any large group, tends to revolve around stories... Confidence is not just the emotional state of an individual. It is a view of other people's confidence, and of other people's perceptions of other people's confidence."

Pause to reflect for a moment on Akerlof's construct "the confidence of a nation." Isn't that what many Canadians rallied to in the election of Justin Trudeau's Liberals in 2015? Canadians who don't necessarily think of themselves as liberals voted Liberal because Trudeau exuded a confidence in the nation that others didn't.

And people's perceptions of his confidence increased their own confidence in themselves. If nothing else happened, our country rediscovered its appetite for story—our ability to tell stories, and to listen and act upon the stories of others.

Surely now is the time to capitalize on that welcome reassertion of Canada's confidence, and to greet head-on the many disruptions that confront us—in our politics and environment, in immigration, law, gender, health, demographics, international relations, you name it. In our economy, let's face it. And in our media, too. Everything has been disrupted, and for that, we need a disruptive narrative.

Ric Young again:[49]

We have coined the term "disruptive narrative" to parallel the familiar concept of disruptive innovation. In both cases, the intent is to have a pattern-altering effect. But whereas a disruptive innovation (the personal computer, for example, or the cell phone) is pattern-altering as it penetrates the market, a disruptive narrative must achieve its impact at a much earlier stage. Long before the possibility has become a reality, a successful disruptive narrative alters our sense of what's possible, and why it's worth pursuing. Disruptive narratives change our sense of—and relationship to—the future. (The same could be said of transformational leaders.)

A disruptive narrative changes the conditions in which publics and stakeholders can pursue bold possibilities by changing the collective imaginary. Boldness must be a key characteristic of the core narratives transformational leaders tell. And indeed, before leaders can convince others of bold possibilities, they must believe in these possibilities themselves. All transformational visions encounter the stout defense of doubt and denial, skepticism and pragmatism. The power of a disruptive narrative is vested not only in the way that it is framed, but in the way it is championed...

A powerful narrative must be shaped. And powerful ways to mobilize it in the public sphere must be devised. Just as brand and reputation management, customer, community and media relations have been internalized as a core competency of modern organizations, we see the management of a core narrative as an essential strategic talent for organizations leading transformative endeavours in today's world.

I share Young's view, but that's easy to do when someone else does the thinking for you. The point, I think, is to honour his cogent and trenchant articulation of why it is so vitally important to be activists for our individual causes, and more powerfully, to be conscious shapers of a narrative that will guide us through what Jane Jacobs once described as our *Dark Age Ahead*. And, to return to the subject of this book, we'll need to devise not just a new narrative, but "powerful ways to mobilize it in the public sphere."

That's what our media are for. That's what we need to do, jointly and severally, if we really want Canada not just to be "back," as the triumphant Liberals would have us believe, but forward. We need to become our own champions again. We need to change the collective imaginary and find powerful new ways to mobilize it so that everyone sees at least some of themselves in Canada's evolving story. To paraphrase Ted Chamberlin, if this is our land, what is our story?[50] Or, to quote Young one last time, and in a way that any good journalist can relate to, "The best story wins."

ACKNOWLEDGEMENTS

WOULD LIKE TO acknowledge and thank the J.W. Mc-Connell Family Foundation for providing me with a senior fellowship in 2015 that enabled me to carry out research for this book. However, to be clear, the views expressed here are mine and mine alone. I would particularly like to thank Stephen Huddart, the foundation's president and CEO, for letting me loose on this subject in the first place.

David Beers, founding editor of the *Tyee*, was a close collaborator and a careful reader whose knowledge and critical eye were invaluable, as was his friendship throughout.

People with more fine-grained knowledge than I have kindly reviewed this work and offered helpful suggestions for its improvement. They contributed their knowledge of the field; provided contacts, articles, papers, and broadcasts; and/or otherwise helped me draw some straight lines through a story that has more angles than a geodesic dome.

Thanks to Beth Haddon, Tim Draimin, Craig Silverman, Mathew Ingram, Chris Wood, Phillip Smith, Penelope

Jones, Anna Mehler Paperny, Delyse Sylvester, Wilf Dinnick, and Christopher Potter in Perugia. In addition, my sincere appreciation goes to the many people named in the text, who agreed to be interviewed and so willingly shared what they know.

I was delighted that Margo Goodhand found sufficient merit in my work to agree to write a foreword. And at very short notice, thanks to Wade Davis, John Vaillant, Ronald Wright, Neil Macdonald, Marie Wilson, Madelaine Drohan, and David Beers for their generous encomiums.

To Rob Sanders of Greystone Books, thanks for your patience—we finally got to work together!—and to your excellent team: Nancy Flight, Jennifer Croll, Lara LeMoal, and designers Will Brown and Nayeli Jimenez.

Editor Eva van Emden brought a light touch but a keen eye and a sharp mind to the manuscript, as did copy editor Amanda Growe.

Yet again, I'm indebted to George Patterson and Josie Osborne for providing a rain forest writing redoubt in Tofino, and for their hospitality. In that vein, ditto Chris Rose and Nancy Knickerbocker, stalwart friends, journalists at heart, and generous hosts. So, too, Ric Young and Louise Dennys in Toronto, inspirational fellow travellers, godparents to my children (heaven help them all), and fellow late diners. In Brooklyn Heights and in the Hamptons, I wouldn't have lasted long without the hospitality of Michael Northrop and Kathy Regan. Likewise Molly Baldwin, in Boston.

I would also like to pay homage to Ben Bagdikian, the legendary American reporter and editor, who did more than most to shine a light on the corrosive effects of media concentration. His landmark book, *The Media Monopoly*, first published in 1983, had seven sequel editions and remains the standard-bearer for anyone interested in journalistic integrity and the protection of journalism as an essential public service. In preparing this book, I tracked Mr. Bagdikian down at his home in Berkeley, California, asking through his wife, Marlene (he was hard of hearing), if he would consider writing a foreword to this book. He replied by email on March 2, 2016:

Dear Mr. Gill,

Thank you for your very kind letter, and yes—I do recall meeting you at the Vancouver convention.

I realize you are under time pressure, but unfortunately I won't be able to comment or add a foreword to your monograph in the near future. However I wish you the best of luck and send warm greetings.

Ben H. Bagdikian

Ben Bagdikian died at home the following week, aged 96, and was remembered in the *New York Times* as "a celebrated voice of conscience for his profession."[1] *Vale*, Ben Bagdikian.

Finally, it was Groucho Marx who once said, "Outside of a dog, a book is a man's best friend. Inside of a dog, it's too dark to read." While I was writing the first draft of this book, my family's beloved dog, Sarge, insisted on taking me for a walk each morning and each evening on Chesterman Beach in Tofino. Sadly, the little guy didn't live to read the final product. Groucho had it wrong. Outside of a dog, or at least a dog like Sarge, a book is no substitute. Not even this one.

NOTES

Introduction: *Requiem mass media*

1. Madelaine Drohan, "Does serious journalism have a future in Canada?" Public Policy Forum, March 2016, 10, http://www.ppforum.ca/sites/default/files/PM%20Fellow_March_11_EN_1.pdf.

2. Jan Wong, "Thousands of cuts in the media industry," Canadian Media Guild, November 19, 2013, http://www.cmg.ca/en/2013/11/19/thousands-of-cuts-in-the-media-industry/.

3. Jim Brown, "Canadian Pulitzer Prize-winning journalist Paul Watson welcomes newsroom closures and layoffs," CBC Radio, February 7, 2016, http://www.cbc.ca/radio/the180/journalistic-darwinism-establishing-ties-with-north-korea-and-alison-sydor-1.3434009/canadian-pulitzer-prize-winning-journalist-paul-watson-welcomes-newsroom-closures-and-layoffs-1.3434048.

4. James Bradshaw, "CRTC to keep tabs on TV networks amid industry turmoil: chairman," *Globe and Mail*, February 17, 2016, http://www.theglobeandmail.com/report-on-business/crtc-to-keep-tabs-on-tv-networks-amid-industry-turmoil-chairman/article28790285/.

5. Journalismis.ca, http://journalismis.ca.

6. Wikiquote, https://en.wikiquote.org/wiki/Conrad_Black.

7. Matt Schudel, "Ben H. Bagdikian, journalist with key role in Pentagon Papers case, dies at 96," *Washington Post*, March 11, 2016, https://www.washingtonpost.com/local/obituaries/ben-h-bagdikian-media-critic-and-journalist-with-key-role-in-pentagon-papers-case-dies-at-96/2016/03/11/9515bb8c-e7bb-11e5-bc08-3e03a5b41910_story.html.

8. Jackie Young, "A study of print and computer-based reading to measure and compare rates of comprehension and retention," *New Library World* 115, no. 7/8 (2014): 376–93.

9. The Aspen Institute, *Informing Communities: Sustaining Democracy in the Digital Age*, (Washington, D.C.: Knight Commission on the Information Needs of Communities in a Democracy, 2009), xiii, http://www.knightcomm.org/wp-content/uploads/2010/02/Informing_Communities_Sustaining_Democracy_in_the_Digital_Age.pdf.

10. Jim Brown, "Paul Watson."

11. Madelaine Drohan, "Serious journalism," 10.

Chapter 1: No Country for Old Media: Our Shrinking Public Square

1. The issue of the *Tofino-Ucluelet Westerly News* that was randomly chosen in the preparation of this book was the November 25, 2015, edition. The number and mix of stories and the amount of advertising obviously vary from one issue to another.

2. David Shedden, "Today in Media History: Mr. Dooley: 'The job of the newspaper is to comfort the afflicted and afflict the comfortable,'" Poynter Institute, October 7, 2014, http://www.poynter.org/2014/today-in-media-history-mr-dooley-the-job-of-the-newspaper-is-to-comfort-the-afflicted-and-afflict-the-comfortable/273081/.

3. Claudia Cattaneo, "David Black's grand vision: Can newspaper publisher from Victoria beat the oil industry to Asia?" *Financial*

Post, June 1, 2013, http://business.financialpost.com/news/energy/david-black-kitimat-refinery-northern-gateway.

4. David Black, "Refinery Proponent Weighs In on Tankers," *Northern Sentinel*, April 2, 2014, 2.

5. Jeff Nagel, "Black touts 'safer' oil-by-rail plan for B.C. refinery," *Terrace Standard*, November 19, 2015, http://www.terracestandard.com/business/351886701.html.

6. Joseph Jackson, "Newspaper Ownership in Canada: An Overview of the Davey Committee and Kent Commission Studies," Political and Social Affairs Division, Government of Canada, December 17, 1999, http://publications.gc.ca/Collection-R/LoPBdP/BP/prb9935-e.htm.

7. *Telegraph-Journal* homepage, https://www.telegraphjournal.com.

8. Bruce Livesey, "Company province, provincial company," *Report on Business*, February 26, 2016, http://www.theglobeandmail.com/report-on-business/rob-magazine/is-the-secretive-irving-family-ready-for-itscloseup/article28917978/.

9. Jesse Brown, "The family that owns New Brunswick," *Canadaland*, November 23, 2014, http://canadalandshow.com/podcast/family-owns-new-brunswick.

10. Richard Valdmanis and Dave Sherwood, "Forget Keystone XL, one of Canada's wealthiest business dynasties has a 'Plan B' for the oil sands," *Financial Post*, March 27, 2014, http://business.financialpost.com/news/energy/keystone-oil-pipeline-energy-east-irving.

11. Jesse Brown, "The Last Newspaper Barons (Live from New Brunswick)," *Canadaland*, February 22, 2015, http://canadalandshow.com/podcast/last-newspaper-barons-live-new-brunswick.

12. Joseph Jackson, "Newspaper Ownership."

13. Ibid.

14. Bruce Livesey, "Company province." (See sidebar "More than fossil fuels and forests.")

15. John Honderich, "Postmedia let down readers by dictating election endorsements: Honderich," *Toronto Star,* November 9, 2015, http://www.thestar.com/opinion/commentary/2015/11/09/postmedia-let-down-readers-by-dictating-election-endorsements-honderich.html.

16. John Barber, "Election deals blow to Canada's dominant press group," the *Guardian,* November 1, 2015, http://www.theguardian.com/media/2015/nov/01/election-blow-canada-postmedia-stephen-harper.

17. Margo Goodhand, personal communication with author, February 28, 2016.

18. John Stackhouse, *Mass Disruption: Thirty Years on the Front Lines of a Media Revolution* (Toronto: Random House Canada, 2015), 92.

19. The *Globe and Mail,* "The Tories deserve another mandate—Stephen Harper doesn't," October 16, 2015, http://www.theglobeandmail.com/globe-debate/editorials/the-tories-deserve-another-mandate-stephen-harper-doesnt/article26842506/.

20. John Barber, "Election deals blow."

21. John Shmuel, "Postmedia Network closes deal to buy 173 Sun Media publications," *Financial Post,* April 14, 2015, http://business.financialpost.com/news/postmedia-network-closes-deal-to-buy-173-sun-media-publications?__lsa=dfae-e69b.

22. Drew Hasselback, "Here's a look at 10 mega-mergers that flushed away billions," *Financial Post,* July 17, 2015, http://business.financialpost.com/investing/buyers-remorse-10-mega-merger-flops-that-flushed-away-billions.

23. James Bradshaw, "Postmedia's S&P credit rating is now the same as Greece's," *Globe and Mail,* December 2, 2015, B2.

24. Paul Willcocks, "As Postmedia withers, is a newspaper-less Vancouver imminent?" The *Tyee,* February 3, 2015, http://thetyee.ca/Mediacheck/2015/02/03/Vancouver-Without-Newspapers/.

25. Competition Bureau, "Competition Bureau will not challenge Post-media's acquisition of Sun Media," March 25, 2015, http://www.competitionbureau.gc.ca/eic/site/cb-bc.nsf/eng/03898.html.

26. James Bradshaw, "Postmedia reports major drop in revenues, Conrad Black scolds leaders," *Globe and Mail*, July 9, 2015, http://www.theglobeandmail.com/report-on-business/postmedia-reports-wider-loss-as-advertising-circulation-revenues-weaken/article25386520/.

27. James Bradshaw, "Postmedia's S&P credit rating."

28. Pete Evans, "Postmedia cuts 90 jobs, merges newsrooms in Vancouver, Edmonton, Calgary, Ottawa," CBC.ca, January 19, 2016, www.cbc.ca/news/business/postmedia-job-cuts-1.3410497.

29. The Canadian Press, "Postmedia CEO Paul Godfrey says firm's debt is like 'a noose around your neck,'" CBC.ca, January 26, 2016, http://www.cbc.ca/news/business/postmedia-paul-godfrey-1.3420505.

30. James Bradshaw, "Postmedia appoints board to review business as GoldenTree seeks an exit," *Globe and Mail*, April 7, 2016, http://www.theglobeandmail.com/report-on-business/postmedia-appoints-special-board-to-review-struggling-business/article29552772/.

31. Kelly Toughill, "Does democracy need newspapers? Maybe not so much," *Toronto Star*, January 22, 2016, http://www.thestar.com/opinion/commentary/2016/01/22/does-democracy-need-newspapers-maybe-not-so-much.html.

32. Pete Evans, "Postmedia cuts 90 jobs."

33. Kelly Toughill, "Does democracy need newspapers?"

34. Chantal Hébert, "Canada's national fabric is paying price for depletion of journalistic resources: Hébert," *Toronto Star,* January 21, 2016, http://www.thestar.com/news/canada/2016/01/21/

canadas-national-fabric-is-paying-price-for-depletion-of-journalistic-resources-hbert.html.

35. Tim Shufelt and Christine Dobby, "Guelph Mercury newspaper to close amid financial pressures," *Globe and Mail*, January 25, 2016, http://www.theglobeandmail.com/report-on-business/guelph-mercury-to-close-amid-financial-pressures/article28370737/.

36. Kate Taylor, "Kate Taylor: Cost of free information could be end of local news knowledge," *Globe and Mail*, January 29, 2016, http://www.theglobeandmail.com/arts/kate-taylor-cost-of-free-information-could-be-end-of-local-news-knowledge/article 28460362/.

37. Shufelt and Dobby, "Guelph Mercury newspaper to close."

38. Dwayne Winseck, "The Growth of the Network Media Economy in Canada, 1984–2014," Canadian Media Concentration Research Project, November 2, 2015, www.cmcrp.org/the-growth-of-the-network-media-economy-in-canada-1984-2014/.

39. The Canadian Press, "Experts on the concentration of media ownership," *Maclean's*, October 6, 2014, http://www.macleans.ca/news/canada/experts-weigh-in-on-concentration-of-canadian-media-ownership/.

40. John Stackhouse, *Mass Disruption*, 87.

41. Margaret Sullivan, "The Search for Local Investigative Reporting's Future," *New York Times*, December 5, 2015, http://www.nytimes.com/2015/12/06/public-editor/margaret-sullivan-new-york-times-public-editor.html.

42. Jonathan Kay, "Charity case," *Walrus*, January 20, 2016, https://thewalrus.ca/charity-case/.

43. Chantal Hébert, "Canada's national fabric."

44. "Royal Commission on Newspapers," Wikipedia, https://en.wikipedia.org/wiki/Royal_Commission_on_Newspapers.

45. Marc Edge, "Convergence and the 'Black News Hole': Canadian Newspaper Coverage of the 2003 Lincoln Report," *Canadian Journal of Media Studies* 2, no. 1 (April 2007), http://cjms.fims.uwo.ca/issues/02-01/edge.pdf.

46. Chantal Hébert, "Canada's national fabric."

47. Jennifer Ditchburn, "Panel of MPs to examine issue of local news crisis, media concentration," CBC.ca, February 17, 2016, http://www.cbc.ca/news/politics/federal-committee-newsroom-closures-1.3451513.

48. "David Frost," Wikipedia, https://en.wikipedia.org/wiki/David_Frost.

49. Margaret Sullivan, "Keep the flame lit for investigative journalism," *New York Times,* December 12, 2015, http://www.nytimes.com/2015/12/13/public-editor/keep-the-flame-lit-for-investigative-journalism.html.

50. Rick Edmonds, "An expert's forecast—Canada will have few if any print newspapers by 2025," Poynter Institute, August 30, 2015, http://www.poynter.org/news/mediawire/368793/an-experts-forecast-canada-will-have-few-if-any-print-newspapers-by-2025/.

51. Ibid.

52. Justin Trudeau, "Minister of Canadian Heritage Mandate Letter," http://pm.gc.ca/eng/minister-canadian-heritage-mandate-letter.

53. Daniel Leblanc, "'Everything's on the table,'" *Globe and Mail,* April 23, 2016, http://www.theglobeandmail.com/news/national/exclusive-canadian-heritage-announces-sweeping-canconreview/article29722581/.

54. Dwayne Winseck, "Media and Internet Concentration in Canada, 1984–2013," Canadian Media Concentration Research Project, November 26, 2014, http://www.cmcrp.org/media-and-internet-concentration-1984-2013/.

55. Dwayne Winseck, "Growth and Concentration Trends in the English-language Network Media Economy in Canada, 2000–2014," Canadian Media Concentration Research Project, December 3, 2015, http://www.cmcrp.org/growth-and-concentration-trends-in-the-english-language-network-media-economy-in-canada-2000-2014/.

56. Steve Faguy, "Media ownership chart," *Fagstein* blog, http://blog.fagstein.com/media-ownership-chart/.

57. James Bradshaw, "The Globe's new home 'a sign of faith in the future,'" *Globe and Mail*, December 18, 2015, http://www.theglobeandmail.com/news/national/the-globes-new-home-a-sign-of-faith-in-the-future/article27879298/.

58. Sarah Marshall, "Why the Globe and Mail is 'incentivising news-room staff,'" Journalism.co.uk, October 8, 2013, https://www.journalism.co.uk/news/-wpe13-why-the-globe-and-mail-is-incentivising-newsroom-staff-/s2/a554375/.

59. James Bradshaw, "La Presse to eliminate 158 jobs, continue transition to digital media," *Globe and Mail*, September 24, 2015, http://www.theglobeandmail.com/report-on-business/la-presse-to-cut-158-jobs-after-axing-weekday-print-edition/article26516549/.

60. Ibid.

61. The Canadian Press, "Toronto Star launches tablet app Star Touch," CBC.ca, September 15, 2015, http://www.cbc.ca/news/business/toronto-star-launches-tablet-app-star-touch-1.3228744.

62. James Bradshaw, "Toronto Star encouraged as tablet app downloads hit milestone," *Globe and Mail*, November 13, 2015, http://www.theglobeandmail.com/report-on-business/toronto-star-encouraged-as-tablet-app-downloads-hit-milestone/article27258635/.

63. Chris Powell, "Star Touch App hits 100,000 downloads," *Marketing*, November 16, 2015, http://www.marketingmag.ca/media/star-touch-app-hits-100000-downloads-161706.

64. Jesse Brown, "Is the News Biz a Lost Cause?" *Canadaland*, January 10, 2016, http://canadalandshow.com/podcast/news-biz-lost-cause.

65. Madelaine Drohan, "Serious journalism," 23.

66. The Canadian Press, "Postmedia CEO Paul Godfrey."

67. Ibid.

68. James Bradshaw, "Torstar continues digital shift amid fourth-quarter loss," *Globe and Mail*, March 2, 2016, http://www.theglobeandmail.com/report-on-business/torstar-posts-loss-as-print-advertising-slide-continues/article28993727/.

69. Kristin Rushowy and Peter Edwards, "John Cruickshank to step down as Toronto Star publisher," *Toronto Star*, March 16, 2016, http://www.thestar.com/news/gta/2016/03/16/john-cruickshank-steps-down-as-toronto-star-publisher.html.

70. John Honderich, "Postmedia let down readers."

71. John Honderich, "Paul Godfrey, get your facts straight: Honderich," *Toronto Star*, January 26, 2016, http://www.thestar.com/opinion/commentary/2016/01/26/paul-godfrey-get-your-facts-straight-honderich.html.

72. Terence Corcoran, "A falling Star: No cash in its dowry, declining revenues and no obvious marriage prospects," *National Post*, February 19, 2016, http://news.nationalpost.com/news/the-falling-star-no-cash-in-its-dowry-declining-revenues-and-no-obvious-marriage-prospects.

73. David Olive, "The problem with Postmedia: Olive," *Toronto Star*, January 30, 2016, http://www.thestar.com/business/2016/01/30/the-problem-with-postmedia-olive.html.

74. Jonathan Kay, "Charity case."

75. Kate McKenna, "La Presse stops printing weekday editions after 131 years," CBC.ca, December 31, 2015, http://www.cbc.ca/news/canada/montreal/la-presse-stops-printing-1.3385321.

76. James Bradshaw, "La Presse to eliminate 158 jobs."

77. Ibid.

78. Simon Houpt, "Rogers cuts 110 jobs, ends all OMNI newscasts," *Globe and Mail*, May 7, 2015, http://www.theglobeandmail.com/ report-on-business/rogers-to-cut-jobs-kill-all-omni-newscasts/ article24306838/.

79. Jan Wong, "Thousands of cuts."

80. Steve Faguy, "The day local TV died," *Fagstein*, December 11, 2015, http://blog.fagstein.com/2015/12/11/the-day-local-tv-died/.

81. Aedan Helmer and Susan Sherring, "CTV co-anchor, CFRA hosts laid off in Bell Media job cuts," *Ottawa Sun*, November 17, 2015, http://www.ottawasun.com/2015/11/17/ctv-co-anchor-cfra-hosts-laid-off-in-bell-media-job-cuts.

82. John Doyle, "Canadian TV, as we know it, is screwed. For now," *Globe and Mail*, November 23, 2015, http://www.theglobeandmail. com/arts/television/john-doyle-canadian-tv-as-we-know-it-is-screwed-for-now/article27440984/.

83. Shufelt and Dobby, "Guelph Mercury newspaper to close."

84. Susan Krashinsky, "Line blurs between online advertising and news," *Globe and Mail*, August 14, 2014, http://www.theglobeandmail. com/report-on-business/industry-news/marketing/line-blurs-between-online-advertising-and-editorial-work/article20070940/.

85. Jessica Reuben, "Why publishers prefer native advertising," *MediaPost*, May 13, 2015, http://www.mediapost.com/publications/ article/249906/why-publishers-prefer-native-advertising.html.

86. Chris Powell, "Postmedia doubles down on native advertising," *Marketing*, April 29, 2015, http://www.marketingmag.ca/advertising/ postmedia-doubles-down-on-native-advertising-144727.

87. Jenny Uechi and Matthew Millar, "Presentation suggests intimate relationship between Postmedia and oil industry," *Vancouver*

Observer, February 5, 2014, http://www.vancouverobserver.com/
news/postmedia-prezi-reveals-intimate-relationship-oil-industry-
lays-de-souza.

88. Madelaine Drohan, "Serious journalism," 10.

89. Jan Wong, "Thousands of cuts."

90. Maureen Dowd, "A penny for my thoughts?" *New York Times*,
November 29, 2008, http://www.nytimes.com/2008/11/30/opinion/
30dowd.html.

91. Madelaine Drohan, "Serious journalism," 11.

92. Tony Wong, "CBC to lose up to 1,500 more jobs," *Toronto Star*, June
26, 2014, http://www.thestar.com/entertainment/television/2014/
06/26/strategic_plan_cuts_hubert_lacroix.html.

93. Laura Kane, "CBC facing backlash from some of its biggest personalities over documentary cuts," *National Post*, June 23, 2014, http://
news.nationalpost.com/arts/cbc-personalities-sign-petition-
opposing-planned-cuts-to-documentaries.

94. Alain Saulnier, "CBC/Radio-Canada in danger of disappearing forever," *Toronto Star*, November 15, 2014, http://www.thestar.com/
opinion/commentary/2014/11/15/cbcradiocanada_in_danger_of_
disappearing_forever.html.

95. Konrad Yakabuski, "CBC has proved it can withstand the axe,"
Globe and Mail, November 26, 2015, http://www.theglobeandmail.
com/globe-debate/cbc-has-proved-it-can-withstand-the-axe/
article27484776/.

96. John Doyle, "CBC needs funding but money doesn't buy smarts
or class," *Globe and Mail*, November 11, 2015, http://www.
theglobeandmail.com/arts/television/john-doyle-cbc-needs-
funding-but-money-doesnt-buy-smarts-or-class/article27214251/.

97. CBC/Radio-Canada website, http://www.cbc.radio-canada.ca/
en/reporting-to-canadians/acts-and-policies/programming/
journalism/.

98. Alain Saulnier, "CBC/Radio-Canada in danger."

99. Canadian Heritage, "Strengthening Canadian Content Creation, Discovery and Export in a Digital World," http://pch.sondages-surveys.ca/s/dwc/langeng/.

100. Simon Houpt, "Blowing up the system to save it," *Globe and Mail*, April 23, 2016, http://www.theglobeandmail.com/news/national/how-will-joly-yank-canadian-media-into-the-21st-century/article29727130/.

Chapter 2 What's Happening Across the Pond?

1. *#ijf16 WebMagazine*, http://magazine.journalismfestival.com/.

2. Ian Gill, "In Italy, Hope, and Some Handwringing, for Journalism," *Tyee*, May 16, 2015, http://thetyee.ca/Mediacheck/2015/05/16/Italy-Hope-Handwringing-Journalism/.

3. Dan Dunsky, "Why Trump is Good for Philosophy," *Medium*, February 29, 2016, https://medium.com/@dandunsky/why-trump-is-good-for-philosophy-9c13164e9f73#.011pj7xpk.

4. Chris Ackermann, "Introducing a WordPress Plugin for Instant Articles," Facebook Media, http://media.fb.com/2016/03/07/instant-articles-wordpress-plugin/.

5. Accelerated Mobile Pages Project, https://www.ampproject.org/.

6. BBC News, "Syrian journey: Choose your own escape route," April 1, 2015, http://www.bbc.com/news/world-middle-east-32057601.

7. Keith Stuart, "Syrian Journey: Why the BBC is right to make a game about the refugee crisis," *Guardian*, April 6, 2015, http://www.theguardian.com/technology/2015/apr/06/syrian-journey-bbc-game-refugee-crisis.

8. Jeff Jarvis, *Geeks Bearing Gifts: Imagining New Futures for News* (New York: CUNY Journalism Press, 2014).

9. Ibid.

10. "Millennials' nuanced paths to news and information," American Press Institute, March 16, 2015, https://www.americanpressinstitute. org/publications/reports/survey-research/millennials-paths-to-news-and-information/.

11. Alex Spence and Joe Pompeo, "The Dutch tech whiz who could save journalism," *Politico*, January 25, 2016, http://www.politico.eu/article/the-dutch-tech-whiz-who-could-save-journalism/.

12. Blendle, https://launch.blendle.com/.

13. "History," Democracy and Media Foundation, http://www.stdem. org/en/history/.

14. James Bradshaw, "News publishers put faith in pay-per-story model," *Globe and Mail*, December 13, 2015, http://www.theglobeandmail. com/report-on-business/news-publishers-put-faith-in-pay-per-story-model/article27741241/.

15. Jasper Jackson, "National daily newspaper sales fall by half a million in a year," *Guardian*, April 10, 2015, http://www.theguardian. com/media/2015/apr/10/national-daily-newspapers-lose-more-than-half-a-million-readers-in-past-year.

16. Dominic Ponsford, "National newspaper website ABCs: Sun fastest growing website in March," *Press Gazette*, April 21, 2016, http://www.pressgazette.co.uk/national-newspaper-website-abcs-sun-fastest-growing-website-march.

17. "The Scott Trust: values and history," *Guardian*, http://www. theguardian.com/the-scott-trust/2015/jul/26/the-scott-trust.

18. "Atkinson Principles," *Toronto Star*, http://www.thestar.com/about/atkinson.html.

19. Alan Rusbridger, interview by Michael Enright, *Sunday Edition*, May 10, 2015, http://www.cbc.ca/radio/thesundayedition/rusbridger-s-campaign-mail-refugees-the-harmonettes-norway-s-9-11-hockey-card-regret-1.3061681.

20. RN, "Guardian Australia funder says site will usher in era of open journalism," February 5, 2013, http://www.abc.net.au/radionational/programs/breakfast/guardian-launches-australian-digital-edition/4500922.

21. John Stackhouse, *Mass Disruption*, 150.

22. Penelope Jones, "The case for the *Guardian* in Canada," shared within personal communication with author, August 2015.

23. "Ashifa Kassam," *Guardian*, http://www.theguardian.com/profile/ashifa-kassam.

Chapter 3 What's Happening Closer to Home?

1. "Walter Gordon Symposium 2015," School of Public Policy & Governance, University of Toronto, http://publicpolicy.utoronto.ca/walter-gordon-symposium-2015/.

2. I attended this symposium, and the quotes and paraphrasing are from my notes on the event.

3. Margaret Sullivan, "Times Reaches Online Milestone, but Many Challenges Await," *New York Times*, August 15, 2015, http://www.nytimes.com/2015/08/16/public-editor/times-reaches-online-milestone-but-many-challenges-await.html.

4. Joanna Slater, "Axel Springer CEO Mathias Doepfner steps boldly into the future of media," *Globe and Mail*, August 15, 2015, http://www.theglobeandmail.com/report-on-business/careers/careers-leadership/axel-springer-ceo-mathias-doepfner-steps-boldly-into-the-future-of-media/article25973668/.

5. Nancy Macdonald, "Canada's prisons are the 'new residential schools,'" *Maclean's*, February 18, 2016, http://www.macleans.ca/news/canada/canadas-prisons-are-the-new-residential-schools/.

6. Erin Millar, "Survey indicates Indigenous people targeted by police in the Prairie provinces," Discourse Media, February 18, 2016,

http://discoursemedia.org/2016/02/survey-indicates-indigenous-people-targeted-by-police-in-the-prairies/.

7. Erin Millar, "Technical Brief: Data journalism about university students' perceptions of police in the Prairies," Discourse Media, http://discoursemedia.org/wp-content/uploads/2016/02/Technical-Brief-Discourse-Media.pdf.

8. "About us: What we do," Discourse Media, http://discoursemedia.org/about/values/.

9. Reporting in Indigenous Communities: http://www.riic.ca/ and http://www.indigenousreporting.com/.

10. "Calls to Action," Truth and Reconciliation Commission of Canada, 2015, http://www.trc.ca/websites/trcinstitution/File/2015/Findings/Calls_to_Action_English2.pdf.

11. "New foundation will foster exchange between religious and non-religious Canadians," Inspirit Foundation, May 3, 2012, https://www.inspiritfoundation.org/application/files/9514/5652/9178/14_Inspirit_Foundation_Launch.pdf.

12. Media Impact Funders, http://mediaimpactfunders.org/.

13. Jessica Clark, "MIF and MIP Team Up to Produce Nonprofit News Impact Guide," Media Impact Funders, June 12, 2015, http://mediaimpactfunders.org/mif-and-mip-team-up-to-produce-nonprofit-news-impact-guide/.

14. Sarah Armour-Jones, "Media Impact Forum 2015: Event Recap," July 1, 2015, http://mediaimpactfunders.org/miforum-2015-recap/.

15. Shan Wang, "Pitching coach: A program at the University of Toronto wants to turn subject experts into freelancers," Nieman Journalism Lab, September 18, 2015, http://www.niemanlab.org/2015/09/pitching-coach-a-program-at-the-university-of-toronto-wants-to-turn-subject-experts-into-freelancers/.

16. "Supporters," Global Reporting Centre, http://globalreportingcentre.org/people/supporters/.

17. "Peter Klein," UBC Graduate School of Journalism, http://journalism. ubc.ca/peter_klein/.

18. "Supporters," Global Reporting Centre.

19. April Lindgren, "Is no news bad news? An investigation of local news poverty in Canadian communities," Ryerson School of Journalism research seminar, November 2, 2015.

20. Local News Research Project, http://localnewsresearchproject.ca/.

21. Ken Doctor, "Newsonomics: In Toronto, The Star is making its own big bet on tablets," Nieman Lab, June 11, 2015, http://www. niemanlab.org/2015/06/newsonomics-in-toronto-the-star-is-making-its-own-big-bet-on-tablets/.

22. Joseph Lichterman, "The Economist's Tom Standage on digital strategy and the limits of a model based on advertising," Nieman Lab, April 1, 2015, http://www.niemanlab.org/2015/04/the-economists-tom-standage-on-digital-strategy-and-the-limits-of-a-model-based-on-advertising/.

23. Marsha Lederman, "TED prize winner to use award to expand oral history project globally," *Globe and Mail*, March 17, 2015, http:// www.theglobeandmail.com/news/british-columbia/ted-prize-winner-to-use-award-to-expand-oral-history-project-globally/ article23514273/.

24. Marsha Lederman, "TED prize winner."

25. Brielle Morgan, personal communication with author, December 2, 2015.

26. Elizabeth Tompkins, "The Best Solutions Journalism of 2015," December 18, 2015, http://solutionsjournalism.org/2015/12/18/ the-best-solutions-journalism-of-2015/.

27. Sharon Pian Chan, "Seattle Times Education Lab shares insights from how it engaged the community in its coverage of school discipline," Knight Blog, December 3, 2015, http://www.

knightfoundation.org/blogs/knightblog/2015/12/3/seattle-times-education-lab-shares-insights-how-it-engaged-community-its-coverage-school-discipline/.

28. "About Us," ProPublica, https://www.propublica.org/about/.

29. "About the foundation," Knight Foundation, http://www.knightfoundation.org/about/.

30. Matter, http://matter.vc.

31. "The Doable City Reader and Series," Discourse Media, http://discoursemedia.org/project/the-doable-city-reader-and-series/.

32. John Bracken and Jennifer Preston, "22 ideas win Knight News Challenge: Elections," Knight Blog, July 22, 2015, http://www.knightfoundation.org/blogs/knightblog/2015/7/22/22-ideas-win-knight-news-challenge-elections/.

33. "Knight Prototype Fund," Knight Foundation, http://www.knightfoundation.org/funding-initiatives/knight-prototype-fund/.

34. The Canadian Press, "Experts on the concentration of media ownership."

35. Emma Barnett, "Is the Huffington Post really worth $315 million?" *Telegraph*, February 7, 2011, http://www.telegraph.co.uk/technology/news/8308631/Is-The-Huffington-Post-really-worth-315-million.html.

36. The Canadian Press, "BuzzFeed to open office in Toronto, establish Canadian editorial team," *Financial Post*, March 12, 2015, http://business.financialpost.com/fp-tech-desk/buzzfeed-to-open-office-in-toronto-establish-canadian-editorial-team.

37. The *Tyee*, http://thetyee.ca/.

38. Rabble.ca, http://rabble.ca/.

39. The *Vancouver Observer*, http://www.vancouverobserver.com/.

40. "About," Ricochet, https://ricochet.media/en/75/about.

41. Ethan Cox, personal communication with author, May 3, 2016.

42. Ricochet, https://ricochet.media/en.

43. Markham Hislop, "The Vancouver School: Inside the B.C. Media's Anti-Oil Crusade," *Alberta Oil*, February 2, 2016, http://www. albertaoilmagazine.com/2016/02/vancouver-observer-the-tyee-energy-projects-bc/.

44. "About Us," iPolitics, http://ipolitics.ca/about/.

45. David Beers, personal communication with author, May 4, 2016.

46. Vauhini Vara, "Survival strategies for local journalism," *New Yorker*, April 15, 2015, http://www.newyorker.com/business/currency/survival-strategies-for-local-journalism.

47. Amy Mitchell, Mark Jurkowitz, Jesse Holcomb, Jodi Enda, and Monica Anderson, "Nonprofit journalism: a growing but fragile part of the U.S. news system," Pew Research Center, June 10, 2013, http://www.journalism.org/2013/06/10/nonprofit-journalism/.

48. Jonathan Sotsky, "Knight's 'Gaining Ground' tracks progress of nonprofit news sites," April 8, 2015, Knight Blog, http://www. knightfoundation.org/blogs/knightblog/2015/4/8/knights-gaining-ground-tracks-progress-nonprofit-news-sites/.

49. Laura Owen, "Pew: Nonprofit news sites are growing, but where's the business model?" Gigaom, June 10, 2013, https://gigaom.com/2013/06/10/pew-nonprofit-news-sites-are-growing-but-wheres-the-business-model/.

50. Tyee Solutions Society, http://www.tyeesolutions.org/.

51. "Hot or fraught?" *Economist*, January 29, 2014, http://www. economist.com/blogs/schumpeter/2014/01/digital-media-start-ups.

52. Tom McCarthy, "First Look Media to launch with Snowden-themed online magazine," *Guardian*, February 6, 2014, http://www. theguardian.com/media/2014/feb/06/first-look-media-online-magazine-snowden.

53. "Frequently Asked Questions," ProPublica, https://www.propublica.org/about/frequently-asked-questions/.

54. Vox Media, http://www.voxmedia.com/.

55. Paul Farhi, "Washington Post closes sale to Amazon founder Jeff Bezos," *Washington Post*, October 1, 2013, https://www.washingtonpost.com/business/economy/washington-post-closes-sale-to-amazon-founder-jeff-bezos/2013/10/01/fca3b16a-2acf-11e3-97a3-ff2758228523_story.html.

Chapter 4 Whither the Future?

1. Gary Mason, "Christy Clark's LNG pledge has yet to pay off, but it may not matter in 2017," *Globe and Mail*, January 4, 2016, http://www.theglobeandmail.com/news/british-columbia/christy-clarks-lng-pledge-has-yet-to-pay-off-but-it-may-not-matter-in-2017/article28009526/.

2. First Call, "2015 Child Poverty BC Report Card," November 2015, http://still1in5.ca/wp-content/uploads/2015/11/2015-BC-Child-Poverty-Report-Card-WebSmall-FirstCall-2015-11.pdf.

3. Lori Culbert, "Care for aboriginal kids 'unsuitable,' 'under-resourced'," *Vancouver Sun*, October 7, 2015, http://www.vancouversun.com/life/care+aboriginal+kids+unsuitable+under+resourced/11422418/story.html.

4. CTV News, "Suffering from residential schools crosses generations," June 2, 2015, http://www.ctvnews.ca/canada/suffering-from-residential-schools-crosses-generations-1.2403786.

5. Ross Beaty, "Forget growth: B.C. needs a steady economy," *Vancouver Sun*, September 23, 2013, A11.

6. Ric Young, "Transformational Leadership in a Time of Austerity" (presentation, Regional Transit Authority Forum, Toronto, ON, May 11, 2012).

7. Tara Deschamps, "Toronto Star and Atkinson Foundation launch 'groundbreaking' philanthrojournalism partnership," *Toronto Star*, October 19, 2014, http://www.thestar.com/news/gta/2014/10/19/ toronto_star_and_atkinson_foundation_launch_groundbreaking_ philanthrojournalism_partnership.html.

8. "Tides Canada partners with The Toronto Star for climate and economy series," Tides Canada, September 17, 2015, http://tidescanada. org/climate-and-energy/tides-canada-partners-with-the-toronto- star-for-climate-and-economy-series/.

9. Stephen Heintz, personal communication with author, June 22, 2015.

10. John Stackhouse, *Mass Disruption*, 282.

11. Jonathan Kay, "Charity case."

12. Jesse Brown, "Walrus violated charity rules, says magazine's co- founder," *Canadaland*, January 31, 2016, http://canadalandshow. com/article/walrus-violated-charity-rules-says-magazines-co- founder.

13. David Beers, personal communication with author, February 2, 2016.

14. Ricochet, "You can boost Indigenous reporting—here's how," August 13, 2015, https://ricochet.media/en/548/you-can-boost-indigenous- reporting-heres-how.

15. Daniel Drache and Fred Fletcher, "Beyond crisis reporting: Rebalancing the relationship with Indigenous peoples," Policy Options, May 2, 2016, http://policyoptions.irpp.org/magazines/may-2016/ beyond-crisis-reporting-rebalancing-the-relationship-with- indigenous-peoples/.

16. Vicky Mochama, "Are Canada's Newspapers Too White? Most Refused to Say," *Canadaland*, March 2, 2016, http:// canadalandshow.com/article/are-canadas-newspapers-too- white-most-refused-say.

17. Margo Goodhand, personal communication with author, February 28, 2016.

18. "Indigenous Media Roundtable," *Canadaland*, February 8, 2016, http://canadalandshow.com/podcast/indigenous-media-roundtable.

19. "Who Are We?" Wapikoni, http://www.wapikoni.ca/about/who-are-we.

20. Christopher Ingraham, "The solutions to all our problems may be buried in PDFs that nobody reads," *Washington Post*, May 8, 2014, https://www.washingtonpost.com/news/wonk/wp/2014/05/08/the-solutions-to-all-our-problems-may-be-buried-in-pdfs-that-nobody-reads/.

21. Shefa Siegel, "Ebola, Liberia, and the 'Cult of Bankable Projects,'" *Ethics and International Affairs*, June 1, 2015, http://projects.ethicsandinternationalaffairs.org/bankableprojects.

22. "Vancouver Foundation becomes the first Canadian community foundation to join the Open Licensing movement," Vancouver Foundation, May 7, 2015, https://www.vancouverfoundation.ca/sites/default/files/documents/Vancouver%20Foundation%20Open%20Licensing%20Announcement%20-%2005-07-2015.pdf.

23. Robert Steiner, "Five Good Ideas about how non-profits can benefit from the media revolution," Maytree, February 2015, http://maytree.com/fgi/five-good-ideas-non-profits-can-benefit-media-revolution.html.

24. Anya Schiffrin and Ethan Zuckerman, "Can We Measure Media Impact? Surveying the Field," *Stanford Social Innovation Review*, Fall 2015, http://ssir.org/articles/entry/can_we_measure_media_impact_surveying_the_field.

25. NRA News, https://www.nranews.com/series/cam-and-company.

26. Hunter S. Thompson, *Generation of Swine: Tales of Shame and Degradation in the '80s* (New York: Simon & Schuster, 1988), 43.

27. Amy Mitchell, Jeffrey Gottfried, Jocelyn Kiley, and Katerina Eva Matsa, "Political Polarization & Media Habits," Pew Research

Center, October 21, 2014, http://www.journalism.org/2014/10/21/political-polarization-media-habits/.

28. John Stackhouse, *Mass Disruption*, 268.

29. Ibid., 282.

30. John Stackhouse, personal communication with author, November 3, 2015.

31. Meghan Smith, "The quotable Tip O'Neill," *Boston* magazine, December 9, 2012, http://www.bostonmagazine.com/news/blog/2012/12/09/quotable-tip-oneill/.

32. "Film and television financing in Australia," Wikipedia, https://en.wikipedia.org/wiki/Film_and_television_financing_in_Australia.

33. Marsha Lederman, "Don't forget Hollywood comes to Canada for the money," *Globe and Mail*, March 4, 2016, http://www.theglobeandmail.com/opinion/the-locale-the-quick-flight-dont-forget-hollywood-comes-north-for-the-money/article29039885/.

34. The Canadian Press, "Postmedia CEO Paul Godfrey."

35. Madelaine Drohan, "Serious journalism," 16.

36. Sylvia Stead, "A parliamentary committee to save the news? Good luck with that," *Globe and Mail*, February 26, 2016, http://www.theglobeandmail.com/community/inside-the-globe/public-editor-a-parliamentary-committee-to-save-the-news-good-luck-with-that/article28930799/.

37. Paul Watson, personal communication with author, February 25, 2016.

38. Phillip Smith, "Dear Media Entrepreneurs: It's time to look north," *Medium*, February 24, 2016, https://medium.com/hacks-hackers-journalism-meets-technology/dear-media-entrepreneurs-it-s-time-to-look-north-189f16bd1edf#.hbbyzaant.

39. IFL Science!, http://www.iflscience.com/.

40. Diply, http://diply.com/.

41. Mitchell Anderson, "IMF pegs Canada's fossil fuel subsidies at $34 billion," *Tyee*, May 15, 2014, http://thetyee.ca/Opinion/2014/05/15/ Canadas-34-Billion-Fossil-Fuel-Subsidies/.

42. Shawn McCarthy and Bertrand Marotte, "Canada's oil industry frets as pressure mounts to cut fossil-fuel tax incentives," *Globe and Mail*, November 12, 2015, http://www.theglobeandmail.com/report-on-business/industry-news/energy-and-resources/canadas-oil-industry-frets-as-pressure-mounts-to-cut-fossil-fuel-tax-incentives/ article27240254/.

43. Kate Taylor, "Cost of free information."

44. Konrad Yakabuski, "CBC has proved."

45. Christine Dobby, "Is high-speed Internet a basic right? CRTC to weigh in," *Globe and Mail*, April 8, 2016, http://www. theglobeandmail.com/report-on-business/is-high-speed-internet-a-basic-right-crtc-to-weigh-in/article29576878/.

46. Sheila Watt-Cloutier, *The Right to Be Cold: One Woman's Story of Protecting Her Culture, the Arctic and the Whole Planet* (Toronto: Allen Lane, 2015).

47. Ric Young, "The Genius of Community," keynote address at York Region Human Services Planning Board community launch, Markham, Ontario, June 21, 2001.

48. Ric Young, "Transformational Leadership."

49. Ibid.

50. J. Edward Chamberlin, *If This Is Your Land, Where Are Your Stories?: Finding Common Ground* (Toronto: Knopf Canada, 2003).

Acknowledgements

1. Robert D. McFadden, "Ben H. Bagdikian, reporter of broad range and conscience, dies at 96," *New York Times*, March 11, 2016, http:// www.nytimes.com/2016/03/12/business/media/ben-h-bagdikian-reporter-of-broad-range-and-conscience-dies-at-96.html.

INDEX

Figures are indicated in italics

DAVID
SUZUKI
INSTITUTE

THE DAVID SUZUKI Institute is a nonprofit organization founded in 2010 to stimulate debate and action on environmental issues. The institute and the David Suzuki Foundation both work to advance awareness of environmental issues important to all Canadians.

We invite you to support the activities of the institute. For more information please contact us at:

David Suzuki Institute
219–2211 West 4th Avenue
Vancouver, BC, Canada V6K 4S2
info@davidsuzukiinstitute.org
604-742-2899
www.davidsuzukiinstitute.org

Cheques can be made payable to the David Suzuki Institute.